# Perilous Times

# Perilous Times

## An Inside Look at Abortion
*Before—and After—*
## Roe v. Wade

Fran Moreland Johns

YBK Publishers, New York

Perilous Times
An Inside Look at Abortion
Before—and After—
Roe v. Wade

YBK Publishers, Inc.
39 Crosby Street
New York, NY 10013
www.ybkpublishers.com

ISBN: 978-1-936411-22-1

Library of Congress Cataloging-in-Publication Data
Johns, Fran Moreland, 1933-
  Perilous times : an inside look at abortion before- and after- Roe v. Wade /
Fran Moreland Johns.
    pages cm
  Includes bibliographical references and index.
  ISBN 978-1-936411-22-1 (pbk. : alk. paper)
  1. Abortion--United States--History. 2. Pregnancy, Unwanted--United States. 3.
Pro-choice movement--United States--History. 4. Women's rights--United States-
-History.  I. Title.
  HQ767.5.U5J647 2013
  362.1988'80973--dc23
                              2013015583

Cover design by Ward Schumaker

Manufactured in the United States of America for distribution in
North and South America or in the United Kingdom or Australia
when distributed elsewhere.

For more information, visit
www.ybkpublishers.com

*This book is dedicated to the memory of Trish Hooper, and to all of the women, past, present and future, who face the complex issue of unintended pregnancy with courage, grace and often insurmountable difficulties.*

# Contents

# Acknowledgments

I am immeasurably grateful to every woman and man who shared stories, and to the many others who offered connections, suggestions, encouragement and good will. Many are named, and many choose to remain anonymous, All together, they and the countless others who work to protect reproductive rights make me hopeful that those rights will somehow be preserved.

This book would never have gotten off the ground without the early support and assistance I received from Helen Hooper McCloskey, Mary Dodge and Lisa Lindelef. My intrepid writers group, Tessa Melvin, Cindy Roby, Diane Rosenblum, Catherine Stern and Deborah Wright heard my own story when I first began to tell it and cheered the project along; the list of others who generously gave their help to me would fill another book.

Help and encouragement also came from past and present board members, staff and/or individual members of reproductive rights groups including NARAL Pro-Choice America (founded as the National Abortion and Reproductive Rights Action League and sometimes referred to in this book simply as NARAL,) Planned Parenthood Federation of America, Trust Women, Medical Students for Choice, Physicians for Reproductive Choice and Health, SisterSong and the Federation of Women's Health Centers. Their backing was invaluable, and deeply appreciated. The tireless efforts of these and other organizations in behalf of women everywhere, especially women without resources or power, also encourages me to believe that those women will not be abandoned.

Lastly I am grateful for my friends and family, who generally wish I would find other things to write about but remain polite. Until motivated to write this book by the death of my friend and fellow storyteller Trish Hooper, I had mentioned my own story to none of them; it was simply something "respectable" women did not do. But my children, Pam Wilson, Sandy O'Brien, Skip and Jill Fossett, and my extended family of nieces, nephews, cousins and assorted in-laws took deep breaths and offered kindness and support. The fact that some of them hold very different views on the subject of abortion yet are willing to talk calmly and listen thoughtfully also gives me hope that this very complex issue will one day come to a just solution.

My limitless love and gratitude go to the Great Encourager, the Senior Editor of Sacramento Street, Bud Johns.

# Introduction

This book has its origins in an unsanitary, illegal, back-alley abortion. Mine. For decades, until beginning work on *Perilous Times*, I never told. Workplace rape – the cause of my unfortunate pregnancy – was hard to prove and rarely spoken of in 1956; abortion was *never* spoken of in polite society.

So we kept our secrets, those of us who survived abortions in the years before Roe v Wade. We rejoiced when laws were challenged and changed, and when the Supreme Court made it official in 1973: women in the U.S. would no longer suffer the shame, guilt, danger and sometimes death that came with the denial of reproductive rights. And we breathed easier. Some remained – or became – activists, while many of us just settled into our varied lives and gave little further thought to the issue.

But the issue itself was far from settled. Along with the rest of the country I read, with shock and disbelief, about the murders of physicians who provided abortion services and others who worked with them. I saw on TV the angry faces of protesters shouting threats and obscenities at women trying to enter abortion clinics. I watched in further disbelief as forces opposing reproductive rights slowly whittled away those rights, state by state, restriction by restriction.

Finally, along with other women who shared my dismay over the relentless march backwards toward the dangerous days we had known, I began to talk. Others, long silent, did the same. We began to share our stories – and our concerns. With all this focus on an undeveloped fetus, was no one considering the woman in whose body it was housed? Would anyone remember our stories? Or care? One of the friends with whom I shared these thoughts was an ebullient, energetic supporter of reproductive rights named Trish Hooper, whose story is told in Chapter One, and whose death inspired the writing of this book.

Women's lives, Trish and I would often say, are at stake.

Women's lives were risked, and often lost, a half century ago, because we did not have the right to choose what happened to our own bodies – and therefore, for reasons that were personal, private and as varied as are women themselves – we took risks that often left us maimed, or dead.

Today, lives are at stake again. The risks, for women as well as for those who work daily to protect reproductive rights – abortion providers, activists, even politicians – never fully disappeared. My story and other stories from generations past are told here in hopes of preserving the truth of those times.

There is a sobering truth of more recent times: similar stories are happening today. In the following pages are stories shared by women from teenage to 40-something who are living at a time when the U.S. constitution protects their right to choose to have an abortion. But because of layers of restrictions or lack of access, they have found it extraordinarily difficult, sometimes impossible, to exercise that right. Or they have managed to end an unwanted pregnancy only after suffering circumstances that caused pain and humiliation not unlike what their mothers and grandmothers experienced.

One young physician spoke of the women she sees in her clinic who, like the doctor herself, have to cross lines of angry protesters shouting insults and obscenities. Her patients are disproportionately poor. Many have health problems that would be exacerbated by continuing the pregnancy, many have more children than they can care for already. And about the protesters she said, "They oppose contraception, they ignore the many vital health services offered at the clinic, they would deny my patients the right to prevent or end an unwanted pregnancy... but they are the same people who would end every program to support these unwanted children."

The fear, shame, humiliation, and emotional and physical abuse being experienced by many pregnant women today are familiar to every one of us who had an abortion before Roe v Wade made it legal. We were not always treated like criminals, but in fact we *were*. For all these reasons we shudder to think it could happen again, that reproductive rights could disappear.

The decision to have an abortion is seldom easy. Of the hundreds of stories I heard during the more than two years spent working on this book, not one involved a casual decision. What each of these women's stories did involve were agonizing days of soul-searching and of very private decision-making – whether they were stories from pre-Roe v Wade or later. As many in the pro-choice movement point out, abortion is morally complex. Few take lightly the fact that human life could evolve from this tiny fetus. Getting into the argument about when life begins was not something the Supreme Court wanted to do in 1973 and is certainly not the wish of this author.

What is beyond argument is the fact that *another* life is involved: that of the pregnant woman. At times, the male involved is also empathetically and otherwise in the picture, as testified to in the chapter of stories told by husbands and lovers. But beyond question is the fact that no one other than the woman can fully know and understand all of the physical, emotional and moral complexities of her particular circumstance. For these women, being told that someone else does know better, and should have the right to dictate what happens to their bodies, is insulting. It can also be dangerous.

The loss of a woman's right to choose is happening. Thirty-nine states have multiple abortion laws. Nineteen of these require abortions when the pregnancy is at viability or over 20 weeks to be performed only in hospitals; most of these also require that the procedure be done only by a physician, and some require a second physician to be present. Twenty-five states mandate a waiting period, usually 24 hours; nine of these have laws that in effect necessitate two separate trips in order to have an abortion. Thirty-six states have laws requiring some sort of parental involvement for minors; 22 of these require consent of one or both parents. Nineteen states mandate counseling before a woman can have an abortion. Such "counseling" can include anything from ultrasound descriptions to discussion of the ability of a fetus to feel pain, to a lecture implying long-term mental health consequences of abortion. The science of these latter two issues is questionable. There are areas all across the U.S. where finding an abortion provider is difficult at best, and getting to the clinic or hospital can require long hours of travel.

If a woman has money and resources she can catch a plane to another city – or another country – for a safe, legal abortion. If she is without money or resources, sometimes if she's unable to afford the time and effort for other reasons, a woman is denied this right. If she is serving her country in the military, where a woman's life can be difficult and rape is not uncommon, her insurance will not cover abortion.

This book is an effort to put a face on some of the women behind the complex decision to end an unwanted pregnancy. It is neither a comprehensive study nor a scientific examination of an admittedly difficult topic. It simply offers a picture of what the dark days before Roe v Wade were like – for women, some of the men who loved them, and others who risked everything in order to help; and of similar times occurring today. Despite the progress that has been made in protecting their health and wellbeing, women faced with unintended pregnancies today can be denied the right to choose a safe abortion, often with disastrous consequences.

The stories told here are true. In many cases names and details have been changed on request, but the stories have come, with very few exceptions, from those directly involved. In no cases other than a few stories from published sources are the women involved more than two or three degrees of separation from me. I have been surprised by the number of women (and men) who said, *"Use my name!* I'm tired of keeping it secret." Many others asked to remain anonymous for understandable reasons, and I have changed names or details of their stories, while keeping as close as possible to the truth told to me by courageous women.

The stories are told because many of us worry that too many women (and men) today have no real image of what those perilous times were like before the right of reproductive freedom was upheld by the U.S. Supreme Court. And we worry about how perilous the times have once again become.

# Chapter One

# Personal Parallel Journeys

I went blindfolded and terror-stricken, as if to an execution. My indomitable friend Trish went eagerly, though with apprehension, to a stark, white room and a waiting physician.

Trish and I were headed, in different years and on different coasts, into the domain of the illegal abortionist before Roe v. Wade. This was where desperate women went to seek help in ending an unwanted pregnancy. Often as not, we had unsuccessfully tried one or another of the do-it-yourself methods rumored to work: douches, terrible-tasting herbal drinks, falling down stairs, inserting various instruments (knitting needles or at times, yes, coat hangers were the most common.) Rumors about these self-help plans were circulated in secret, but the results could become very public when the method failed, as was too often the case. The woman seeking an abortion started her day much as Trish and I started ours. At the end of the day she might be blissfully un-pregnant, possibly hospitalized and in pain, and occasionally dead. Trish and I lived to tell the tale, but of course we told it to no one for decades. Illegal abortion stories were too filled with guilt, shame and horror to tell, and we were too busy trying to stuff the whole experience down below our conscious memory even to consider bringing it to light.

One early conversation with my friend Trish Hooper changed all that for me. "You had an abortion back then?" she asked. "Well, of course I did, too. We just didn't talk about it. Nobody did. And nobody today understands how grim those days were." The stories of our very different but similarly traumatizing abortions in the days before Roe v. Wade often bookended Trish and my conversations about public affairs and private concerns. And it often ended with one of us saying, "We really ought to write this down. No one will remember, no one will understand." Then one day Trish died, and I found myself saying, "Who will remember? Who will understand?"

For some women today, understanding those old days is easy. They may not remember them as traumatic, personal experiences; women born in the U.S. after the late 1950s never lived through a time when abortion was illegal. But an increasing number of them are experiencing the same hardships that women knew before Roe v. Wade: desperate to end an unwanted pregnancy, agonizing over an endless variety of reasons not to bring an unwanted child into the world, they are discovering they may have little choice. Take the case of the 37-year-old, widowed mother of four who, in 2009, became pregnant despite having taken multiple precautions. She lived in a state where abortion is heavily restricted and no clinic was within a day's travel. Her immediate fear was that her pregnancy would become too advanced before she was able to obtain a safe procedure, and that fear led her to a potential solution many activists believe is already common: the do-it-yourself medical abortion. A friend helped her secure misoprostol, a drug commonly used for gastric ulcers, which she believed would cause her to abort the fetus. Lacking proper information and care, she soon was bleeding heavily, in pain and now seriously afraid. The woman drove 300 miles to a hospital emergency room in another state, where a surgical procedure ended both the pregnancy and the bleeding problem. "She told me it had been the scariest week of her life," said the physician who shared this story. "The decision to end the pregnancy had been painful and hard, because she loved her children and was even hoping eventually to marry the man who had impregnated her. But for all of their sakes she felt she could not have another baby at that time. She said she would make the same decision again, but would try very hard to find a better way to end the pregnancy."

It was a story not unlike that of feminist author/activist Carol Downer years earlier. Downer was the mother of four children and in the process of getting a divorce from their father when she realized she was pregnant. It was some 10 years before the passage of Roe v. Wade.

"The actual process of deciding to have an abortion was pure hell," Downer says. "I spent weeks talking to friends, counselors—my husband would even have been willing to get back together. I was just under horrific pressure to make a decision. One moment I would say 'I love my kids—I could welcome another child into the world' and the next morning I'd wake up and look at what a hardship it would be for me and the kids. We were very broke.

"I had gone to work in a typing pool when I separated from my husband. A woman there who had a lot more information than I referred me to a doctor on Central Avenue in Los Angeles." The neighborhood was unfamiliar, one known more for high crime than sterile clinics. "I got my husband to go with me. I went to the address my co-worker had given me, and was led into a small room by a woman in a white uniform. She disappeared and the doctor—I presume he was a doctor—came in. I had had four kids, and was familiar with it all: the table, the stirrups, and he seemed to know what he was doing. It began to be incredibly painful, though, far outstripping delivery pain, and it went on and on. When he finished he said to call in three days and gave me a phone number. I had left the kids with my grandmother, and when I got home I just fell into bed. I remember waking up, and I could hear the birds chirping and was just so glad to be alive. After three days I called the number he had given me. He said, 'I packed your uterus to prevent hemorrhaging, and you must now pull it out...'"

Downer survived that experience—one of the most painful of her young life—with no permanent damage. Would she make the same decision again? "Unquestionably!" She was soon deeply involved in the women's liberation movement, embarked upon a distinguished career as an author, an immigration lawyer and founder of the Federation of Feminist Women's Health Centers—and she did indeed later welcome two more children of her own into the world. Her concern today is that women could again endanger themselves for lack of access to safe abortion.

Trish Hooper was an activist for a long list of progressive causes, the author of a memoir titled *I'm 87 and You're Not* and for many years the writer of articulate, impeccably crafted letters to editors of publications ranging from the *New York Times* to the *San Francisco Chronicle* to *Time Magazine*. When she died, the opinion section of the *Chronicle* carried a full-page testimony to her wit and wisdom, with a sampling of letters including this one:

"My views on abortion had never been formed one way or another, when on a day way back in 1946—to my horror and my dismay—I realized I was pregnant. Abortion? That was a word overheard; a procedure not understood; an act not allowed by law, difficult to come by and physically dangerous. Whispers told about the devastation to your psyche, your mind, your heart, your body. But you knew that no matter what you'd have to go through, you'd go through that hell, take all the risks, to be unpregnant again. That has always been true, generation after generation.

"What I hadn't expected was this: the enormous gratitude, the relief, the fact that the world was turning again in the sun, once the procedure had been completed, and by an understanding doctor. During those long dark years before abortions became legal and safe, in 1973, unplanned pregnancies often ended in butcheries, with young and older women maimed, many dead. This will happen again, of course…"

When unplanned pregnancy happened to Trish she was a young, vivacious, beautiful 19-year-old, in love with the handsome Naval officer-to-be whom she would soon marry. She had grown up in a prominent San Francisco family, gifted intellectually and athletically; among other things, she was an accomplished horsewoman. Much later, she wrote about what followed the discovery that she was pregnant:

"After a week or three of frantic emotions, trying this and that with no success I finally decided to try riding. I called the St. Francis Riding Academy which was out near Geary and about 26th, I think. Grandfather kept a big old tough gelding there with a really rough mouth and a disposition which rivaled father's when he was angry. He kept his big western saddle there too. I often rode with him, on an English saddle, and I never had the same horse but usually a good ride. That day, I asked the man in charge to get my grandfather's horse ready for me with English saddle. He tried to steer me onto something gentler, but I stuck to my choice, hung up and drove out to the stables. The big horse was waiting, chewing on his bridle, shifting from foot to foot, already with spittle on his mouth. He hadn't been ridden for a while and clearly didn't want me on his back, but there I was. We finally got out of the stable and onto the street with the horse awkwardly side stepping down the road. After some trouble getting across the busy intersection into the park, away we went. My idea was to ride as fast as possible and fall off at a good place where surely I would be knocked out of being pregnant. We careened down towards the bay and as we passed the waterfall across the road I pulled the big horse up abruptly. He reared and down I went, hitting the ground hard. The horse, with his reins still in my hand, stood trembling, overheated and about as scared as I was.

"There was very little traffic because of gas rationing, but a car with two men in it stopped and offered to help. I was firm and polite, and asked them to hoist me back up. Covered with dirt and aching all over, I turned the horse around, thanked the two men, and headed home. I don't remember much about getting back. I knew I was a total mess. The men at the stables wanted me to call home and have someone come for me, but I refused." Trish drove home, carrying her scrapes and bruises with her.

"Mother took one look at me and put her hand over her mouth and called the doctor. I told her I'd fallen off because I had a sudden dreadful pain on my right side and probably had appendicitis. She called someone she knew, a nice Jewish doctor who shooed mother out of the room. He sat down next to me on the bed and immediately asked, 'Do you think you're pregnant?' I said yes, and burst into tears both of shame and of relief. After a moment, he said, 'Do you love him? Do you want children?'

"I said yes to both questions. He then gave me the routine examination, said yes, I was about 5 or 6 weeks along and he would remove my appendix the next morning. I asked him how much he felt he had to tell my mother. I remember that he just looked down at me for a moment or two, took a deep breath and said he hoped my appendix wouldn't give me any problem.

"Mother drove me to the hospital. She must have known, but neither of us said anything of any importance. John had already left for Officer's Training in Maryland. I never told him. My relief, and my gratitude for the doctor who could have lost his license, cannot be overstated. I was not interested in that 'thing' which was causing me to rethink my entire life." But rethinking, Trish wrote many years later, led to the marriage, family and active life she might otherwise have never known.

My own experience, ten years after Trish Hooper's wild ride through Golden Gate Park, was a continent away and frighteningly different. I would have flung myself off of a dozen horses had I been able to find them. I was 23, three years out of college, still new to the big city of Atlanta, totally inexperienced in matters of sex and ways of the world, and unbelievably naïve. I was working in what seemed the ultimate glamour job, doing oil industry public relations that involved things like setting up conferences in fancy resort areas and then hanging out to write press releases in between the cocktail parties and banquets. The events were favorite pastimes, under the guise of industry business—and some productive work did indeed get done—of rich and powerful corporate executives. It was a heady time.

I had grown up in a close-knit family in the central Virginia town of Ashland, which still maintains the highway sign noting it is The Center of the Universe. Throughout the 1940s and '50s, doors were left unlocked, the pace was slow, life was good and everybody in town knew the business of everyone else. My father was president of Randolph-Macon College and my mother the perennial chairwoman of almost every happening at Duncan Memorial Methodist Church. By the time I finished college and set out for Atlanta, Ashland had begun to shed its provincialism but not its pride; a scandal in the Moreland family would have been problematic to a daunting degree. Pregnancy before marriage? No matter the circumstances, I would have jumped off a bridge before even discussing such a thing with my upright parents.

The man was married, widely influential in social, business and political circles and in a position to wield substantial power over my life. He was known as a womanizer—to everyone, it seems, but me. I had learned to handle mild flirtation but knew nothing about self-defense. I was single and hard-working, intoxicated with freedom and the limitless possibilities ahead. I had a full and exciting life, a promising future in my chosen field of writing/public relations and every intention of soon settling down to the wife-and-mother role then essentially the sole accepted and universal American-girl dream. For these and a long list of other reasons, not least of which was my proper, church-going family a few states to the north, there was no way in the world I could consider having a baby.

I drank paregoric, hurled myself against walls and did, for a while, all the other terrible things rumored to end a pregnancy. Many of the most dangerous I had fortunately not yet heard of—the drugs and potions that caused permanent sterility or worse—but everybody knew about the coat-hanger. I have no idea how I managed not to kill myself with the coat-hanger. Finally, thoroughly terrified, I decided that I could not do it myself.

I turned first to my trusted physician. He suggested immediately that I find a way to marry. If not the father, he said, then someone else. Barring that possibility, he said he could direct me to a discreet, out-of-state place where I could go at minimal cost, have the baby and put it up for adoption. It would only be six or eight months out of my life, he said, with a wave of his hand. Losing half a year of my life, having to live a lie for the rest of time and never mind the shame and grief that would still befall my family—the prospect held no attraction that my 23-year-old mind could discern.

I told the man who had impregnated me. He seemed hardly bothered. Later on, his indifferent attitude and cavalier stance would fuel my rage, but only much later on; at the time I felt only fear. He told me to talk to a woman who worked in his same building, assuring me that she could tell me what to do. Only *much* later would it occur to me to wonder how many times he had played out this scene. Our encounter would today be easily classified workplace rape; in those days leading up to the Women's Liberation movement any such accusation or protest would have been laughingly dismissed.

I had casually known the woman to whom I was referred. She was sexy and sophisticated in a worldly-wise way I suspected I would never be; and I was right in that, at least. I told her I had a friend who needed an abortion. She wrote down a number on a slip of paper, told me to call and ask for Barney, said not to worry. It'll cost $100, she said. My salary at the time was $190 a month and my savings account totaled about $27. I went back to the man involved, who said he'd have the $100 for me the next day—that afternoon, if I needed. What I needed was a lot more than money; but empathy, compassion and a sterile abortion were nowhere available at the time. I went to a pay phone and dialed the number.

A woman answered the phone. "Sure," she said, "he's right here." Barney came on the line and asked me who knew.

"Nobody," I said.

"OK," he said, "can you get $100?"

"I have it."

Barney said to be in front of the Loews Grand Theater on Peachtree Street at noon the next day, a Saturday. "Alone," he said. "If it looks like anyone might be watching or following you, the deal is off and there will be no second chance."

I stood in front of the Loews Grand Theater that day in the icy February rain, as alone as I had ever been in my life, waiting for a black 1952 Buick sedan. Barney pulled up, quickly reached back and opened the rear door, and pulled off as soon as I was halfway in. He handed me a musty, blue-flowered bandana, folded into a blindfold.

"Tie this around your eyes," he said, "and sit in the middle of the seat. Have you got the money?"

"Yes."

The atmosphere of the car suggested it might have been closed up in damp, mildewed spaces; there were a few, sad peanut hulls on the floor. As I tied the bandana—as loosely as I thought I could get by with—around my eyes it felt as if I were transporting myself into some stale, foreign never-never land.

For the next twenty minutes we drove in silence around the city, slowly doubling back from one block to another, working our way toward a part of the city I seldom visited but nevertheless knew fairly well. A co-worker lived in that part of town, and Atlanta at the time was not the sprawling metropolis it would soon become. We entered an area of faceless pre-fabricated houses that had been hastily put up for returning GIs a decade earlier. I had twisted the blindfold slightly when I tied it on, leaving plenty of space on the right side to enable me to sneak glances and keep track of where we were headed. Those houses have long since fallen down or been bulldozed, but I could drive you to the exact spot any day, now more than fifty years later. Even at the time I noted the irony of driving eastward out Moreland Avenue. When we got into the neighborhood which was our destination, Barney spent another good five or ten minutes slowly circling, sometimes stopping briefly by an empty field where he could see across to an adjacent block. It would have been hard to tail him, but if anyone were trying, Barney was darn well going to find out.

Eventually we pulled into the carport of a small, dreary, gray ranch-style vinyl siding house and Barney said I could take off the blindfold. Those were the first words he had spoken since "Have you got the money?"

The carport door led into a drab, dingy kitchen, where the woman stood. Steamy and overheated, it smelled like last night's fried food and boiled greens. She took the money. Barney disappeared. The woman pointed me into a small room that led off a short, dark hallway just beyond the kitchen, told me to put my coat on the chair and remove my panties, Barney would be here right away. In the room was a wooden table similar to the one in my parents' kitchen. There were two chairs and another, smaller table on which there was a pitcher of water alongside a basin, some paper cups and a small stack of towels. The room had faded wallpaper with rows of brownish designs that looked like stalks of wheat.

Barney entered, minus his overcoat. He could have been anyone's bad caricature of a greasy-haired and down-at-the-heels salesman. He had on a white shirt and red striped tie, both pretty much the worse for wear. Had I not been hypnotically bound into it myself, the entire scene would have seemed something so like a bad B movie as to be funny. It was not funny at the time. Barney said to lie on my back on the table. This won't hurt, he said. I felt something being inserted into my vagina, something smaller than a tampon. It was over in a matter of minutes. Barney said to put my panties back on and he'd be in the car. I wondered later if he had bothered to wash his hands, before or after.

As he drove me back to the Loew's Grand, Barney said I should expect to start bleeding within a few hours. That was the extent of our conversation, but the trip back took only a fraction of the time spent driving out.

Barney was right about the bleeding. I told my roommates I was having some really bad cramps, and thought I'd stay in bed on Sunday. Monday morning I was still bleeding heavily and more than a little frightened. I called my physician and said I needed to see him right away. I told his receptionist that I had been ice skating and had a bad fall. When I got to the waiting room I was surrounded by confident-looking young women, a few visibly pregnant and wreathed in smiles. What must it be like, I wondered, to have such self assurance—and control? Would they know what to do if their pregnancy were not a blessing but a horror? I felt, for my own part, that I must have a scarlet 'A' on my forehead. The receptionist handed me some forms to fill out and said, "didn't you just see the doctor last week?" It sounded like an accusation.

The doctor said, "Who did this to you?" "Nobody," I said, "I just went ice skating and had a bad fall." After a few moments of uncomfortable probing, verbally, emotionally and physically, he said, "You are one of the lucky ones." He gave me a prescription to fill and told me to come back in a month, sooner if I had problems.

And it turned out to be true, I was one of the lucky ones. I lived to marry in a long white gown, and to raise three children who every day of their lives have brought me enough joy to overshadow any memory of bad times before or since. Except this memory does not go away... and I still mourn for those who were not among the lucky ones.

There were two other options open to women desperate to end an unwanted pregnancy beyond Trish's experience with a courageous— some would say foolish—physician and mine with a back alley butcher. She could go to another country, or she could attempt to do it herself. Women with money and resources chose the former; women without such advantages often took the latter route. Many did not survive. It is the likelihood of a return to these choices that fuels the fight for reproductive rights still raging in the U.S. As access to safe, legal procedures becomes more and more difficult, women with resources will find competent physicians; the disadvantaged will find back-alley abortionists or risk injury or death by trying to end a pregnancy themselves. Or they will bear a child they cannot support, whose own life is likely to be harsh.

The saddest of these stories will never be fully told; snippets and sketches and rumors are all we have. A 67-year-old woman from Texas told me, "There was a girl in my high school senior class. One day she was simply gone. It was called 'a tragic death from accidental poisoning,' but her best friend knew she had been pregnant." An acquaintance of mine e-mailed, "My co-worker in Cleveland died suddenly in a private hospital, in 1971. Her family was in New Jersey; they called me because I was her immediate boss in a large department store. The cause of death was listed as 'sepsis.' A doctor friend explained that sepsis could come from a lot of things, but in young women it was very often the result of a botched abortion. I would have given anything to have been able to tell that family what happened to her. But knowing the whole story might very well have hurt more than it helped."

Dorothy, a friend of mine who was also close to Trish, did not want her real name used because she never shared this story with her children. It is, though, an example of some of the happier outcomes experienced by more fortunate women.

In the mid-1960s, Dorothy and her husband Dick were settled into a new home in a northern California city with their four young children. He was already a prominent researcher; she was a stay-at-home mom. Both were deeply committed to helping those less fortunate, and Dorothy was already launched into causes in the areas of education, minority and women's rights that would be the focus of her entire life. When they discovered she was pregnant again, they felt the added stress would be dangerous. "We already had our family," she says. "There was no way we were going to go through with this pregnancy."

Abortion at the time was "a little bit legal in California," Dorothy says. "You had to have two psychiatrists determine that you might be suicidal if you didn't get an abortion." This option was chosen by others, Dorothy knew, but "Dick had learned about the potential issues that could arise, and the circumstances under which my medical records might be opened." They decided to ask, in strictest confidence, a very good friend who was a physician. "So we asked him over, saying we just wanted to talk with him. After we told him the situation, we asked where I might go that would be medically safe. He said, without the slightest pause, 'Oh, you could go to the same person my wife went to.' That was the end of any fear I had."

Within days, Dorothy and Dick had completed arrangements to fly to San Diego, where they joined a small group of women, most accompanied by husbands or boyfriends, all having pre-arranged to make the trip. "We were picked up by a taxi that had been fitted with extra seats," she says, "and were driven across the border to Tijuana. The clinic itself was clean and nice, and I felt very safe. We didn't know what to expect—but then, I had not expected my doctor friend to have the names, phone numbers and everything else we needed. The cost was $500, which was a *lot* of money in those days; only people with money were able to do this."

Sometimes, as detailed in a later chapter, the experience of accompanying a wife or girlfriend who was having an abortion was almost as traumatizing for the man involved. Not so for Dorothy's husband Dick and the other men in their border-crossing expedition. "You know the 'Longest Bar in the World,' at the Tijuana Mexicali Beer Hall?" Dorothy asks. "They waited for us there. Even though I was never fearful or in pain, the experience was very hard and very stressful for me. But for the men? I don't think they suffered a bit."

The men at the Long Bar may not have suffered, and the cavalier Romeo behind my own horror story all those years ago certainly never showed even a minimal sign of remorse. But others did. They stood shivering on street corners, forbidden to accompany their wives or lovers into the realm of the abortionist, wondering if they would ever see their lovers alive again. They worked nights and weekends to pay off exorbitant fees charged by abortionists who operated outside all laws or regulations. You will meet some of them in later chapters as this tale continues.

And as for the women? There were many, many fortunate women like Dorothy a few decades ago who, for reasons ranging from serious to imperative, were able to end an unwanted pregnancy in relative safety. Because continuing the pregnancy would damage their families, ruin their careers or be destructive in many other ways, they quietly arranged for sterile procedures to be done in secret by trusted physician friends, or they traveled to carefully researched facilities in other countries. Women without money or resources followed other, dangerous paths.

Over and over again, while collecting stories and comments for this book I have heard from physicians, activists and thoughtful, often extraordinary women, "It's going to happen again. It's already happening." Denial of access, restrictive and punitive state laws and the lack of physicians willing or able to perform abortions have brought about situations in many states not unlike the days before 1973. Progress in education and contraception, seen by many as key to reducing the need for abortion, is uneven. And sadly, unwanted pregnancy still happens.

It happened to Rachel in 2009. "There just wasn't anybody within 100 miles who would perform an abortion," she told me. "My regular doctor said he could not help, he did not perform abortions. Even though I was barely six weeks. The more I searched for a clinic, the more I got referred to sites that sounded likely but then turned out to be what I call tricksters. When I called on the phone, they would initially sound pleasant and sympathetic. Several did not want to talk beyond an introduction and said I would have to come in to the clinic to get more information; others, when I said I was not interested in adoption or prenatal care information, would turn unfriendly very quickly. One actually said, 'You do realize you are talking about killing a human being?' I didn't see it that way. I thought of it as a bunch of cells that could become a human being, maybe. But for now it was a part of me that I had come to terms with losing. It wasn't as if I hadn't thought it all through, and it made me mad that this girl acted like she knew better.

"I knew of a drug that my boyfriend said he could get, so that's what we decided to do. I just thought there was no way I could go through with this pregnancy. I don't know exactly how he got the drug, but I trusted him. Pretty soon after I took it I did start bleeding, but it never did quite stop. I went back to my regular doctor, and he sent me to the emergency room at the county hospital, where they admitted me and did a D&C. As it all turned out I was fine, and not pregnant any more. One nurse at the hospital was very sympathetic, though she told me they all knew what I had done. Another used those same words about how I had 'killed my baby.' It made me mad all over again."

Rachel has plenty of company in her anger. In state after state, as restrictions are piled on restrictions, women feel deprived of a consti-tutional right by those whose religious or political views are at odds with that right. Abortion providers, worn down by restrictions layered on top of restrictions and often fearful for themselves and their fami-lies, wonder how long they can keep doing what they were trained to do as a part of comprehensive women's health care. One told me, "On days I volunteer at the clinic, something I still love to do, it's hard not to wake up angry." I asked if she worried about people like my 1956 abortionist getting back into the business because legal options in so many states are becoming fewer and fewer. She said, "I hope not. I hope to God not."

# Chapter Two

# How Did We Get Here?

In the beginning—or soon after the beginning—there was abortion. People had sex when procreation was not intended, pregnancy happened, and attempts were made to end the pregnancy. In all probability, women tried to end those pregnancies in ways not far different from the do-it-yourself abortions of more recent years.

First century women had access to herbs like pennyroyal, which was described nineteen centuries later by botanist/writer Margaret Grieve as "an old-fashioned remedy for menstrual disorders." Early opinion-makers like writer/naturalist/philosopher Pliny the Elder of ancient Rome knew that the silphium plant would "promote the menstrual discharge." Women of 8th-century India were advised to sit over a steaming cauldron of stewing onions. Through the ages, in ancient Latin, in Sanskrit, probably in cave writings, women have passed along these "remedies." If they were around to tell their stories, they would undoubtedly report that the silphium/pennyroyal teas and assorted other remedies brought widely mixed results. Sometimes they included sickness and death.

Through the ages there have also always been abortionists, some motivated by compassion, and some entering the field for less honorable reasons. In 19th century New York, news reports suggested they numbered in the hundreds. Whatever their unconfirmed numbers, the most notorious was a woman named Ann Lohman who, as the flamboyant "Madame Restell" defied Victorian convention, the police, and Anthony Comstock. Comstock, organizer of the New York Society for the Suppression of Vice, led a campaign against all things he considered lewd, immoral and—specifically—sexually improper. Made a special agent by the Postmaster General, he ended the career of Madame Restell decades before birth control pioneer Margaret Sanger ran up against the eponymous Comstock Laws.

But before committing suicide rather than face a second jail term, Madame Restell offered abortions to the women of New York for nearly 40 years beginning in 1839. She might have lived and died without incident but for the luxurious lifestyle her business success allowed and the flamboyance with which she enjoyed it. Repeatedly accused and arrested, she drove from the brownstone mansion she had built on Fifth Avenue to the courthouse for required appearances in a coach and four. The time she did spend in prison, in 1848, was reportedly eased by a feather mattress and other comforts of home. The lavish nature of that confinement prompted an investigation of the alderman said to be responsible, but he suffered little more than briefly being scandalized and Madame Restell, meanwhile, was back in business. Her services included not only abortions but also provision of birth control and occasional lying-in rooms for women whose babies she would then place with adoptive mothers. But her career and life came to an abrupt end when Comstock, posing as a potential client, received both contraceptive supplies for himself and his lady and the offer of an abortion if needed. Rather than face another trial and likely jail term, she slit her throat on April 1, 1878 in the bathtub of her Fifth Avenue mansion.

If Madame Restell was in business primarily for the comfortable lifestyle that her rich clients could provide, the woman who followed her onto the New York scene a few decades later was motivated by the plight of the poor. And would have a far more significant and lasting impact on the world.

Margaret Sanger was the first American to force the issue of abortion onto the public conscience. Much the same as with advocates for choice today, she was honored by progressives, vilified by the religious right and vehemently opposed by groups across the conservative spectrum. Before Sanger began the crusade that would lead to the foundation of Planned Parenthood, most abortions took place either under the empathetic eye of the family doctor—if he was willing—or, more often, far outside the range of any medical knowledge or proper care. Sanger did not set out to make abortion available; she wanted to make it unnecessary; it was prevention of unwanted pregnancies that she sought—and that got her in trouble.

Born in Corning, NY in 1884, Sanger was one of eleven children of a Roman Catholic mother (who died of tuberculosis when Sanger was twelve) and a free-thinker father. Her mother's early death and her father's radical nature provided a good foundation for her own chosen path, and the fact that her mother endured eighteen pregnancies over thirty years made an indelible mark. "My mother died at 48," Sanger wrote. "My father lived to be 80." After taking nursing training in White Plains, NY, she moved to New York City and began working with poor women on the Lower East Side. It was there that she saw the often horrific results of do-it-yourself abortions gone wrong. The story goes that Sanger accompanied a physician on an emergency visit to the home of a woman named Sadie Sachs. Sadie had three children and a truck-driver husband named Jake, and was desperately ill from a self-induced abortion. Sanger nursed her back to health. When Sadie, barely recovered, pleaded with the doctor for help to avoid another pregnancy, he suggested that she "tell Jake to sleep on the roof." Not long afterwards Sanger responded to another emergency call at the Sachs home, where Sadie died in her arms from another botched attempt to self abort.

The Sadie Sachs story is grounded in fact but was likely embellished over time. "Grandmother," says author/Planned Parenthood International executive Alexander Sanger, "never let the facts get in the way of a good story." But in her autobiography Sanger paints a vivid picture of Sadie and Jake and the tragedy of their circumstances. She recounts numerous tales of women desperate to end unwanted pregnancies one way or another, drinking herb teas or turpentine, inserting slippery elm, begging pharmacists (or Sanger herself) for anything to help them. Most wound up with raging infections or uncontrolled bleeding that, more often than not, killed them. That Sanger repeatedly saw the results of botched attempts to self-abort unquestionably led to her conviction that families should be planned and women should have control over their own bodies. A woman's choice of whether or not to bear children, and how often, she saw as "a fundamental freedom."

Margaret Sanger's own views were never gentle or moderate, and her more outspoken opinions are often used against her. "No woman can call herself free," Sanger wrote, "who does not own and control her body. No woman can call herself free until she can choose consciously whether she will or will not be a mother." Sanger believed that sex should be mutually satisfying or should not happen, and that women must stand against the state, the church, and any other institution that would presume to dictate the affairs of women's bodies. But she also spoke out loudly and frequently enough about peripheral family planning issues—she said two children per family are plenty, those with physical and emotional wherewithal to raise children should have them and those without should not—that she stands accused of everything from bigotry to supporting eugenics. Neither accusation is precisely correct, or deserved. What is indeed correct and worth celebrating is her remarkable success in bringing the issue of women's reproductive rights into the open—and in helping millions of women around the world avoid the fate of Sadie Sachs.

In the early 1960s, half a century after Sanger's work began to offer choices to women with unwanted pregnancies—and to make giant strides toward pregnancy prevention and improved health in general—a similarly dedicated young woman worked for the Planned Parenthood League of Massachusetts in Boston. Pamela Lowry had left college at 19 and quickly landed a job she found meaningful. She was hard-working, passionately committed to helping others, and possibly more naive than wise. Part of her job involved fielding calls from desperate young women who were seeking ways to end unwanted pregnancies, and their stories tore at her heart. In the 1960s abortion was illegal and thus not an option. "We could counsel women about how to avoid getting pregnant, but in those days could not teach them about safety," Lowry says now, "I had to have that conversation privately, on the phone, at home. I used to tell women, 'If you're going to seek an illegal abortion, there are some things you can do to increase the safety level, but PPLM only deals with contraception. If you call me at home, however, I can share what I know as a private individual.' PPLM provided no clinical services, but could refer people for pregnancy testing, which often led to finding other problems or to the welcome discovery that the woman was not pregnant after all." After its founding in 1970, PPLM began referring people to Pregnancy Counseling Service, which in turn often referred them to the Clergy Consultation Service described later in this chapter. PPLM eventually did begin to provide information about abortion possibilities overseas.

At some point, though, Lowry's heart was tugged a little too hard, and it led her to make an empathetic but unwise move: she gave her home phone number and the promise of help to a distraught young woman caller. It was help that PPLM could not and did not give. After doing some extensive research of her own, though, Lowry had finally found someone who performed abortions.

"Pretty soon," she says, "one call in the middle of the night became several, and eventually I was getting them every day." The innocent gesture soon became a system, with Lowry connecting desperate women to the trusted doctor through a trusted driver. And for a while it was a system that worked to the benefit of many women without danger to them, or much of a hitch. But one day Lowry came home to find a letter in her mailbox: *Dear Pamela*, it began; *First of all, let me sincerely apologize for involving you in this unpleasant matter. Unfortunately, it has become necessary to do so...*

The unfortunate matter was blackmail, and the anonymous sender had done his homework carefully. Detailed in typed letters that Lowry kept in a manila envelope over the following decades, the episode reads today like a plot for a B-grade crime movie; at the time it was an idealistic young woman's worst nightmare:

> A few weeks ago, my sister came to me for financial aid for an abortion. She learned of the doctor through a former abortionist whose operation had been exposed. I gave her the money, and the operation was (as she reported) well executed in pleasant surroundings.
>
> Unknown to my sister, I followed her, and consequently uncovered the entire operation. I had previously sent my fiancée to have an abortion (through YOUR $600 set-up: a friend had told me about you.) Anyway, between my sister and my fiancée, I have spent $1600 on abortions. I did not have this money, and was forced to drop out of school to pay the loans.
>
> I know every detail of the entire "abortion ring." "Eddie" picks up the girls in a cab, and then he is met somewhere (once the Museum of Science) by "Gene," who is Eugene Cheek of 6 Grape Street in Malden—he drives a gold 1966 Pontiac Bonneville, MASS license #659-540. "Eddie," "Gene" and the girls arrive at the house,

112 Franklin Street in Malden. The house was recently purchased by one Francis Sugarman of 105 Bainbridge Street in Malden. The names of two single girls are listed as residents, one of whom may be "Sally," another member of the operation.

Upon the night of my fiancee's abortion, I was not surprised at the elusive route taken. I hid nearby, and got an excellent infrared photograph of the doctor emerging from the front door. (The doctor has NOT YET been further identified.)

In the first of what would be an escalating series of threats the blackmailer appends an inked message with an arrow to the 'not yet'— *DON'T LET IT HAPPEN!* Then he gets back down to business:

> Anyway, this is not black mail. I have much respect for you, Pamela, and I will not do anything to expose this operation unless I am forced into it. All I want is my money back!

To that end, the self-proclaimed not-a-blackmailer goes into underlines and all-capital-lettered instructions:

> TONIGHT, FRIDAY, SEPTEMBER 29. EITHER (BUT NOT BOTH) "EDDIE" or "GENE" will bring $1,600 in CASH— LARGE BILLS in a plain envelope to: Ken's Restaurant in Copley Square. I am 6' tall, black hair, brown eyes, and will wear a bright red shirt. I will be just inside the door, standing at the delicatessen take-out counter at EXACTLY MIDNIGHT. I will wait fifteen minutes, NO LONGER. If one of them has not shown up with the money by 12:15, I will leave. I will immediately proceed to mail (via registered letter) five letters. Each will be a copy of ALL THE INFORMATION I HAVE MENTIONED, plus your (Pamela Lowry) name, address, affiliation with Planned Parenthood League, and the abortion set-ups. Letters will be sent to the Mass Medical Society, Malden Police, AMA, The Boston Globe and the Planned Parenthood League.

Then follows a typed, red ALSO and a further message suggesting that the writer, despite his respect and appreciation for Lowry, was not above fearing she would promptly hire a hit man to take him out:

> I have specific arrangements to meet my sister at a certain time and place thereafter. If I do not show up FOR ANY REASON, THEIR COPIES OF THE SAME LETTERS WILL ALSO BE MAILED, along with a notification to the police of my disappearance.

The letter concludes with further assurances that all he wants is his money back, and the hope that they will all be more careful in the future. He hopes they all understand his sincerity and position—but

> God help the bunch of you if you don't comply. P.S., Pam, don't show your face anywhere around Ken's tonight, or the mail goes out. Someone who knows you will be watching for you.

Lowry remembers the day as not one of her best. She met with the doctor, who called a meeting of his group. "I felt terrible," she says, "but I told them I thought it was legitimate, and asked them to meet the bribe. We all agreed this was the thing to do, and trusted it would be a one-time-only thing." However, matters did not proceed quite as smoothly as hoped. The appointed courier showed up at the restaurant at the appointed hour with the cash, but the blackmailer never appeared. Instead, another letter soon came in the mail:

> PAMELA: You really didn't expect me to meet you at Ken's. THE MEETING WILL TAKE PLACE ON TUESDAY MORNING (OCT.3) AT <u>EXACTLY</u> TEN A.M. I will be wearing a hat, glasses, a black suit and a red tie. I will be standing just inside the front entrance of THE BOSTON POLICE DEPARTMENT, STATION FOUR (7 Warren Avenue, near the corner of Berkeley and Tremont Streets...)

More instructions followed about handing over the cash, don't say a word, don't even think about trying to identify me because *if at any time in the future "foul play" is attempted on me, my lawyer has instructions to open a sealed packet which will contain the usual information letters to be mailed.* And he took the trouble to add, *I am not a criminal, and am within the law in trying to retrieve my money. I honestly feel your Service is damnably necessary, and I would sincerely regret exposing you, if you force me to do so...*

It was one blackmail letter too many. Lowry had her phone number changed, went to Planned Parenthood President Loraine Leeson Campbell and poured out her story. "She immediately picked up the phone and called a friend on the Massachusetts Supreme Court, who got me a good Catholic lawyer so that if the police arrested me I could say, 'I want to talk to my lawyer.'" These were the good old days of live telephone operators, which turned out to be helpful. "I got a phone call, after I had unlisted my phone number. The caller identified herself as an operator (which I truly believe she was). 'Someone is trying to reach you who says they have a medical emergency and must speak with you,' she said. 'May I connect them?' By pure coincidence, there had been an article in the paper recently about a young woman who lived on the north shore who was arrested for marijuana possession. Her name was the same as mine, Pamela Lowry. I suspected the police might be behind this 'medical emergency' call so I quickly took advantage of the other Lowry's misfortune. 'I'm sorry, operator,' I replied, but I think this a case of mistaken identity. There was someone who is also named Pamela Lowry—some woman on the North Shore—who was arrested recently in a drug case. I suspect this 'medical emergency' call is someone who is in need of drugs and is trying to get hold of the woman who was arrested.'"

In fact, the system had worked quite well for a period of time, to the benefit of many women. They were taken to the home of a woman who was a nurse, and the $600 fee was divided as follows: $100 to the nurse, $100 to the driver, $400 to the doctor. (Lowry was in it for the goodness of her heart.) Immediately following the attempted blackmail, all of these stopped providing services of any kind and assumed very low profiles. But on November 1, 1967, the *Boston Herald Traveler* ran a small story on page 33 reporting the arrest of three men (including the doctor) "accused of conspiracy to commit unlawful abortions."

Lowry felt it the better part of wisdom to leave the country. The fact that she was madly in love with her future husband, who had recently moved to Paris, added to the attraction of the idea. She spent an entirely blackmail-free year in London, working at a Family Planning Association office. Among other events of that happy year she participated in giving H.R.H. Prince Philip a tour of Margaret Pike House, the FPAs flagship of a model birth control and sex education clinic, in Her Majesty's hometown.

One man interviewed for this book was an undergraduate at Harvard in those days, and first became aware of the Planned Parenthood League while working on a student booklet about health resources. He had only a dim recollection of the events detailed above but he well remembered the organization and the people. At the end of our brief conversation he added this comment:

"Pam Lowry? The people at PPL? Those were the heroes."

Decidedly not a hero was an abortionist active in the Washington/ Baltimore area at the same time, the man encountered by Roz Jonas. Jonas grew up to be a leader in the fight for abortion rights, serving on the board of the National Abortion and Reproductive Rights Action League (NARAL) and in key positions with other progressive causes. As a young woman in the suburbs of Washington, D.C. in the turbulent 1960s, she would not have predicted such a course. She was living at home with her highly respectable Jewish family, working for a Congressman on Capitol Hill and enjoying a pleasant relationship with her first serious boyfriend. She was 19. Her first sexual experience, with that first boyfriend, resulted in a pregnancy that threatened to tear her peaceful world to shreds.

"I called a friend at Goucher College," Jonas says, "and through a network there she got me the name of a physician to see. That physician confirmed my pregnancy, and gave me a piece of paper and sent me off to what I presumed to be another physician." "I was told to be in front of a movie theater in downtown Baltimore. My boyfriend left me there. I had had to ask his parents for the $600, which was just terribly humiliating. I stood in front of the theater, alone. Eventually a man with a dog came up to me; I don't know if I thought he was a serial killer." She went with the man, into a car which traveled from the meeting place all the way across rural Baltimore County; they had little conversation other than his saying, at one point, "there were supposed to be others." Their trip ended at an isolated farmhouse. They were met there by a couple who led Jonas into a room equipped with a bed with stirrups. "After a time, a man came in, wearing a surgical mask," Jonas recalls. "I was not asleep, and I was terrified. He finished without a word, and the woman came back in to help me get dressed. After she gave me a little package with some pills, the same guy drove me back to Eutaw Street."

Another story from these days gives additional insight to the complexity of pre-Roe pitfalls for many young women. Constance had an abortion in 1956, the same year as I did. Mine was in urban Atlanta, hers in rural Maine. "I lived in a very small town," she says. "Everybody knew everybody, but not everybody knew that my uncle's widely respected business partner and close friend was a sexual predator. I didn't exactly know it myself, even after he molested me the summer after I graduated from high school. I was 17 and unbelievably naive. My mother had died when I was 12 and I had no brothers or sisters, just my father. I loved him very much, and I think he loved and respected both his brother and the business partner—who was a few years younger than my father. I felt somehow at fault. The man swore it was out of undying love for me, that he was simply unable to restrain himself. He swore it would never happen again, and begged me not to tell anyone because of all the damage to our families, his business, everyone's reputation that would result. I remember feeling like everybody else had to be considered and I didn't matter all that much.

"When I discovered I was pregnant I went to see the man and told him I didn't know what to do. He had the unmitigated gall to ask if I were sure 'he was the one.' In a way that was fortunate, because it made me so furious it gave me courage. After I gathered my wits about me I assured him there had never been any other, and said if he couldn't find a way to help me I didn't see anything else to do but tell my father. I told the man I would be glad to tell my uncle too, although that was really a bluff; the idea of telling my uncle was something harder than I could possibly even imagine.

"It took him (the rapist) all of one day to come up with the solution. He told my father and my uncle—I was beyond lying at this point and could not have said a word—that I was going to help him with some business matters. We drove to a city about two hours away, to the office of a doctor my abuser apparently knew. He performed the abortion, I got back in the car and we drove home. Aside from the fact that being in the car with this man was an assault all by itself, the experience was not that bad. I played the car radio very loud the whole trip. I knew I would be leaving for college soon, and the few times I saw the man after that I just tried to stay on the other side of the room. I do remember that as a dark time.

"In the early 1960s there was a story in the papers about an abortion ring having been exposed in that city. I recognized the name of the man who had performed my abortion. I remember feeling enraged about the whole thing. Not because I thought these doctors were bad people, but because I thought the ones who should have been brought to trial were the predators who brought 'patients' like me for them to take care of. For years after Roe passed I beat myself up over what I hadn't said and hadn't done, but I'm over that now. I've told the story to my husband and children, the man is dead and I don't even hate him any more. Most of all, I am proud to have a daughter who is an Ob/Gyn and works with a Planned Parenthood clinic."

Abortion rings, including some with qualified physicians willing to take risks for reasons both honorable and less so, flourished in many major cities prior to Roe v. Wade. Not all were quite such cloak-and-dagger operations as Pam Lowry's turned out to be, as seemingly safe and open as the one to which Constance's abuser delivered her, or as secretive and humiliating as the one Roz Jonas' experienced.

In many cities around the country, there was reliable help. An organization known as Clergy Consultation Service, still remembered with gratitude by many women over 60, operated fully aboveboard and was carefully protective of the health and safety of women seeking to end unwanted pregnancies. They may have skirted or occasionally broken the law, but "The Law" would have had its hands full going after a group with the prestige, respect and widespread support of these distinguished community leaders.

Now-retired minister Dr. G. Clyde Dodder was in San Francisco during the city's free-wheeling 1960s. "Some time around 1967," he says, "my wife went to a seminar in Berkeley, at which an African American man spoke about the problems (of unwanted pregnancies) that were being experienced. My wife came home and said, 'What are you going to do about it?'—and I didn't know. About the same time, I received a letter from a church in Greenwich Village on the same subject—women with unwanted pregnancies having nowhere to turn—and right after that letter arrived, we moved from California to Boston. I was a Unitarian at the time. I got in touch with the man who had sent that letter—his name was Howard—and we started finding doctors who were willing to do abortions even though it was illegal and frowned upon by the institutions they were associated with. It was suggested that we organize churches to counsel women. We got together people from a lot of different churches—Unitarian, Congregational, Episcopal, Presbyterian and others—to talk about this problem. Somebody suggested—it might have been me—that ministers ought to make themselves available to counsel women needing abortions. So we started a group in Boston, and word got out pretty quickly. We had groups throughout New England."

Dodder's wife, a nurse, was running a free clinic at the time and understood clinical needs. She would go out to inspect the clinics to which women would be directed, in places like Montreal, London and Mexico City. "There was a Dr. Fernando in Mexico City who owned his own clinic and it was perfect: everything very sterile, highly educated nurses, it was excellent."

Doctors in the U.S. did join forces with Clergy Consultation in occasional underground groups. "In Boston at the time," Dodder says, "it was even difficult to get birth control. We got in touch with a loosely organized group of liberal young doctors who had gotten together to talk about these issues. Through these younger doctors we got in touch with other, really established doctors associated with the major hospitals." If abortions were actually performed at these institutions or by these physicians, it was at a major risk—but filled a huge need. "We set up a telephone line," Dodder recalls, "with a number that women could call. It was headquartered at my church in West Newton, and we had a volunteer at the church—a woman who had needed an abortion herself. It was incredible how much need there was, and how quickly word spread. At one time the minister at Arlington Street Church—an historic Unitarian Universalist Church in downtown Boston—told me he saw 12 women in one day, all asking for help."

There were other such groups in many major cities. The Clergy Consultation Service had its actual beginnings at Judson Memorial Church in Greenwich Village under the leadership of Rev. Howard Moody, who was in all probability the man who had written to Clyde Dodder. Founded by 21 ministers and rabbis to counsel women with unwanted pregnancies, CCS spread to include similar groups like Dodder's Boston operation. Its work was augmented by underground networks like 'Jane' in Chicago and Patricia Maginnis' widely used referral service in the San Francisco area. In 1973, they all gratefully went out of business when the passage of Roe v. Wade ended the need for their mission. Many of the doctors and lay people involved in these late-1960s movements were also key figures in the movement to legalize abortion itself; some of their stories, and more of Maginnis and the women of the Jane organization are in later chapters

More than a few people working for reproductive rights today fear the need for such groups could return. They include abortion providers and activists whose stories are told in later chapters; some of these activists had illegal abortions themselves and some have more recently become involved. Most of them agree with Roz Jonas' comment that "it is a dangerous time for choice."

How dangerous? A woman's right to choose, though constitutionally guaranteed, has all but disappeared in some states. Free choice has been replaced with layers of restrictions and lack of access that make abortion virtually impossible for all but those who are financially well off. As a result, the choice can become one of either attempting to self-induce—often with tragic results—or bringing an unwanted child into the world. Since welfare and child-care opportunities in these same states also tend to be ungenerous, the subsequent life of that unwanted child can be equally tragic—which widens the field of those who look both backward to how we got here and forward to where we're going. A physician volunteer at a Planned Parenthood clinic which has been targeted by anti-abortion protesters for many months put it this way: "I am a healthy woman fortunate to have been raised in middle-class comfort. An abortion I had at 19, after a failure of birth control, was safe and without problems, so I did not have to derail my college and graduate school training. All I want now is to provide less advantaged women with the same good health and, when needed, the same choices that were mine. Performing abortions is only a tiny part of what goes on at our clinic. What we're doing is keeping women—and their partners—healthy and helping them prevent unwanted pregnancies from happening so they don't *need* abortions. Plus, we're doing a lot of really important things like mammograms and testing for STDs and education. I've been yelled at by protesters who thought I was coming for an abortion, and by others who recognized me as a doctor. I get that they believe abortion is wrong. But what's not to love about all the other work we do at the clinic that benefits their community?"

Harry Jonas, MD (unrelated to Roz Jonas in the earlier story) shares that distress. Jonas is now retired from a long and distinguished career that included nine years as dean of the University of Missouri-Kansas City School of Medicine and 13 years as assistant vice president for medical education at the American Medical Association. A tireless advocate for family planning and reproductive rights in his home state and across the nation, Jonas believes that there are countless other physicians in his generation who feel just as strongly as he, because they witnessed the tragedies of botched abortions before Roe v. Wade. One such tragedy sticks in Jonas' mind more than a half-century later.

"I was doing a residency in Ob-Gyn," he says. "I had a woman come in who had had 14 pregnancies and had 12 living children. She had performed a self-induced abortion because she had not been able to find a doctor who could help her. She was desperate because she had a 'troublemaker' husband who was gone most of the time and she told me, in the emergency room, that she could not raise another child. She said she could not feed another child. She had perforated the vagina and the uterus with an instrument of some kind and her intestine was coming out of her vagina. She had massive infection, multiple abscesses in all of her organs. She died within 48 hours of admission, despite vigorous treatment. I still remember that patient. I remember exactly what she looked like. I remember the bed she was in on Ward 1418. I will never forget it."

Jonas is disturbed by "the way the issue has been taken over by people who don't want to see any sort of family planning at all. When I was practicing prior to Roe v. Wade I was very involved in the family planning movement. But when women would come seeking information about abortion the only thing I could do other than break the law and perform an illegal abortion—which I didn't do—was try to get them somewhere else where they could get something done, usually another country. But I was practicing in a very blue collar community where people weren't affluent and couldn't afford to go to Tokyo or Stockholm or wherever. Many of them ended up with illegal abortions, and many of them died. For 25 years prior to Roe v. Wade in my home state of Missouri, the most common cause of death in women of child-bearing age was infection from illegal, self-induced abortion."

# Chapter Three

# Good Guys, Bad Guys:
# The Illegal Abortionist Up Close

"Do I think the illegal abortionist will be back? Without a doubt. If we keep going down the road this country seems to be on, it's sure to happen." A young obstetrician-gynecologist only a few years past her medical training and now working as an abortion provider at a women's health clinic, offers these words. "It won't be the same as 50 years ago, and hopefully there won't be as many crude and totally unsafe situations. But as more and more restrictions are layered on top of each other in many states, or if the anti-abortion forces succeed in overturning Roe, illegal abortionists will be back in business. Some for humanitarian reasons, some for the money. It won't be *much* money, because women with money can go to another state or another country. But less-advantaged women desperate to end an unwanted pregnancy are going to find ways to end it. If people are around to help them, trained or untrained, it won't matter, they will seek those people out."

Helena (a pseudonym), a young, soft-spoken abortion provider in one of the states with heavy restrictions, made a comment that sums up much of what her colleagues around the U.S. have been saying: "If you want to know what the illegal abortionist looks like, and what illegal abortion will look like, go to Kenya." Helena had recently returned from working for six months at a hospital in Nairobi. She was one of four Ob-Gyn physicians with whom I talked, over the several years of working on this book, who had spent time within that East African country, in one area or another.

Kenya has a population (according to 2010 census data) of close to 40,050,000, in an area of 219,788 square miles—about twice the size of Arizona or Nevada. The birth rate in recent years has averaged well over 30 per 1,000 people, nearly three times that of the U.S. Coming up with an estimate of how many women are injured or killed by backstreet abortionists—or in attempts to self-induce—is an impossibility. But physicians who have worked in women's health there say it would be a staggering number. "They don't have any options," Helena told me. "Wealthy women can go to a private physician, undergo counseling and have an abortion, essentially just circumventing the system because abortion is only legal under strictly limited circumstances—rape, incest, if the mother's life is in danger. Poor women literally by the thousands try to self-abort, or go to untrained abortionists. What are these people like? I can't tell you precisely because I never met one; but my guess is that they are both women and men who have learned rudimentary practices and built reputations by word of mouth. They may have minimal compassion but not much; I only saw their botched jobs. In the time I was there I saw a number of women who were critically ill, either with raging infections or with puncture wounds from illegal abortions. I was told that such instances are very, very common. But for all the obvious reasons you don't see the women in hospitals unless and until the situation is critical. (A Guttmacher Institute report estimated that there were 317,000 abortions performed in Kenya in 2002, and 21,000 women were admitted to public hospitals with abortion-related complications. Poor women, the study reported, generally had no way of knowing whether their abortionist was trained or safe.)

"Women in Kenya," Helena says, "will try anything to end an unwanted pregnancy, much as women in the U.S. did before Roe. I don't think the people who do the backstreet abortions are necessarily terrible people, although I guess most of them are more interested in making a quick buck than in helping a desperate woman. It's just sad, because they are untrained, unregulated and often unsafe."

Illegal abortionists in the U.S. before 1973 were similarly unregulated and unsafe. They were also untrained, with the exception of sympathetic physicians who felt women should have better choices, and the few unscrupulous physicians who were in the business for money. (A few stories about the compassionate, often well-trained volunteers in groups such as Jane in Chicago and on the west coast are included in a later chapter. Some women members of these groups were also providers of illegal abortions.) Helena thinks we will see many of the same things again if abortion is criminalized. Just as there is no certainty of their reappearance in the future, there is no data on illegal abortionists in the past. What follows, though, are snapshots of a few of them.

Illegal abortionists in the U.S. before 1973, as is true of their present-day counterparts in Kenya, were not all evil people. Admittedly, they were committing a crime; they were taking women's lives into often inept and uncaring hands. But these men—and a few women—who are forever inked into that grim, pre-Roe v. Wade history as "back-alley butchers" were not always deserving of condemnation. They were, to thousands of women, a welcome, last-resort solution to the difficult problem of unwanted pregnancy. And they existed only because of the need for some solution. If a few were actually caring and compassionate and some could be seen as downright evil, most of them were unremarkable people who were unhindered by personal morals and willing to break the law to make a quick buck. People you would customarily avoid like the plague—unless you happened to find yourself with no other option.

Barney, the abortionist in my own story told in Chapter I, was probably a classic Bad Guy. My doctor's advice, either to marry somebody—anybody, fast—or go spend the next six or seven months in some forlorn home for unwed mothers, had left me frightened and angry. In a sense I felt that Barney had given me my life back. My abortion was crude and unsterile, and probably a closer call than I realized at the time, but since I managed not to wind up permanently maimed or dead I hold no particular animosity toward Barney and his accomplice, the woman who took my money when I arrived at the abortion site. Later, when my doctor pressed for information about "who did this to you?" I was ready to go to jail myself before leading the police to the home of that unsavory couple. I think they were flawed human beings putting desperate young women at risk just to make money.

But I did not consider them outright evil at the time, nor do I consider them particularly evil all these years later.

I didn't get much of a look at Barney. Not only was I blindfolded, more or less, while we drove around Atlanta in circles, I didn't *want* to look at him. Nevertheless, once the blindfold came off I formed a lasting picture of him that remains undimmed all these decades later: slicked-back dark hair that could have used a shampoo. Grungy white shirt with collar and cuffs somewhat frayed around the edges. Dark blue suit, of the polyester fabric popular in the 1950s, the kind that got shiny in spots if it were worn long enough. And a red tie. I remember having the impression that Barney looked as if he would be more at home working almost anywhere other than in an abortion business—but then, my personal experience with abortion businesses was, happily, limited to that one small room in the dingy little house with vinyl siding.

Pictures of other illegal abortionists have emerged as the stories told here unfolded. There was the grim-faced, stocky woman improbably dressed in a flowered apron with ruffles over the shoulders, whose image remains etched into the memory of my friend Elizabeth, as told in detail a few pages later. There was a doddering octogenarian with shaky hands, encountered by a terrified abortion-seeking woman who stammered out that she had changed her mind and fled the room. She managed to find someone slightly less frightening a few days later, and had an abortion without problems. About the elderly would-be abortionist she turned down, she has this to say: "I think he was a retired doctor who had fallen on hard times and turned to performing illegal abortions as a way to make ends meet. Maybe he had done them for many years. The room was in his home and seemed quite well equipped. But when he walked in and I saw how old he was, and that his hands were literally shaking, I fled. He had white hair and a trimmed beard, was clean enough, and dressed in a suit with a vest. There was a white lab coat hanging on a stand in the corner. I guess he changed into it when he went to work. But the man had Parkinson's or something similar and God knows how fast he could have perforated my uterus. I know I should have turned him in to the police, but I was acting just as far outside the law as he was. By the end of that week, and those experiences, I just wanted to put it all behind me and get on with my life."

As to the others, there were endless varieties of sleazy men in rumpled suits, looking anxiously over their shoulders, or hurrying to get their clients out of the building and themselves safely back on the road to anonymity. None of them could be considered motivated by compassion, although some showed a kind of businesslike concern for their clients. Most of them were presumably in it for the money, as the cost of an illegal abortion before Roe v. Wade was equivalent to well over $1,000 today. Someone averaging just three or four clients per week, therefore, could make a pretty good living. Unfortunately, though the overhead was low, many believe the mortality rate among those clients tended to be pretty high. There is no data to back up this assertion. There are only the stories of those who survived and those who worked for women's rights a half-century ago, along with the stories of the physicians today who struggle to preserve those rights.

Fortunately, professional and compassionate help was indeed available before Roe v. Wade for some women with unintended pregnancies. There were underground networks of physicians willing to risk everything, and there were safe options in other countries for those with money and connections (each discussed in later chapters.) There were tightly-held communications about physicians who would help certain groups. The artist Judith Clancy, whose widower I married in 1992, found a caring doctor in Pennsylvania in the 1950s reportedly well known to a widespread circle of creative women. This may well have been the same Pennsylvania Ob-Gyn whom a writer friend described with affection and gratitude a half-century later:

"What I remember most vividly was the kindness of the doctor and his nurse. I knew, and I knew they knew, that they were taking a huge risk to help me. They knew only that I was frightened, alone and had come close to doing myself harm before a friend of a friend told me how to contact them. The doctor kept saying, 'You mustn't be afraid any more. You mustn't worry. You're going to be just fine.' He was a short, gray-haired man with spectacles that made his eyes seem large and bright. He told me he had practiced medicine for decades, 'and until recently no one tried to tell me what I could or could not do for my patients. I am still simply trying to do what my patients need, and to give them best possible care.' I had heard so many horror stories about terrible back-alley abortionists, and here was this grandfatherly person just trying to help me. I was pregnant by a man who I thought loved me, but he disappeared the day I told him I was pregnant. I think the abortion doctor immediately sensed my despair, because he seemed so intent on comforting and reassuring me. I can't think of him at all as a criminal, only as someone angry with the system and determined to help women he thought needed good care."

But for hosts of frightened, desperate women without such resources, unsavory characters were the only available option. The lucky ones like me drew someone whom we hoped never to see again but who was, at the very least, competent enough not to kill us.

The Flowered Apron Abortionist, her client Elizabeth and I agreed in a gallows-humor conversation fifty years later, would make a fine villain for an eponymous crime novel, though neither of us plans to write it. "There was nothing remotely funny about her—or anything else within that scene—at the time," she says now. "But the whole episode is permanently lodged in my brain, and it could at least prove that truth is darker than fiction. Partly because it was a life-changing experience, with a roller coaster of emotions rocking my young life," she says now, "I have willed it into my subconscious. But I have forgotten virtually nothing."

The storyline of Elizabeth's experience is much the same as many others that were encountered as this book evolved: a phone number from an acquaintance who said she had gotten it from another friend, a meeting at some very public spot—in Elizabeth's case it was the side entrance to a downtown department store in her medium-sized southern town—followed by a circuitous drive to a remote property that she says must have been a family farm. "The house was just off a two-lane state highway about 15 miles outside of the city limit, in an area that was mostly small farms at the time but has long since been swallowed up by the city. The man had handed me a blindfold to tie around my eyes—which I did, though I could see out of the corners. I knew approximately where we were going. It was not an area I was familiar with at all. We pulled up almost to the door of the house, and he said I could take off the blindfold.

"She was standing at the door, The Flowered Apron Abortionist. I thought she might be his wife, or some sort of partner, maybe even an out-of-uniform nurse. She was ordinary-looking and unremarkable, except for the flowered apron which just seemed totally out of synch with what was going on. Huge red and orange flowers. She was tall and big-boned; it was not becoming to her."

"So, were you scared, or comforted?"

"I think neither. I just wanted to get it over with. I guess maybe I was a little reassured when I realized that she was the one doing the abortion, as the man had not seemed a very sympathetic or attractive character.

"Flowered-Apron led me into a small room featuring a bed with stirrups." She took my jacket, pointed to a chair, said: 'Underpants. There.' And I swear those were the only words she uttered until it was all over. The man had already taken my $200. Flowered Apron left the room for barely three minutes, returned as I was sitting on the edge of the bed, motioned me to lie down, inserted a straw or some sort of a small tube into my vagina (apparently a crude but common method of inducing abortion, possibly with something else introduced through the straw), handed me a packet of pills, told me to put my pants back on and left the room. I never saw her again. The man was waiting at the car. I climbed in the back seat, closed the door behind me and was whisked back to the department store. He did not hand me a blindfold this time. Maybe they figured once you've actually had the abortion there's not much chance you're a plant.

"I think because everything happened so quickly it still seems a bit surreal. But afterwards I began having terrible cramps and bleeding and it turned really scary. I was in the hospital for a week with bleeding, infection and a raging fever. I started to hate her a little then. I still do. I eventually finished school and had a pretty good career, but it took years of therapy to come to terms with all of those emotions. Behind them was my rage about the boy involved (I never saw him again either) and against the system that forced me to take such a dangerous path. And in the end that was what led me to become a volunteer with organizations working to make sure women now will have a better choice."

Some of the abortionists who flourished in the days before Roe v. Wade were, like Barney and the Flowered Apron woman, merely unsavory characters. And some of them were truly evil. One phone interview with a prominent physician/writer introduced me to this reality:

"Ask them if they had to give sex." Dr. Malcolm Potts said. He offered this as an immediate first suggestion about collecting women's stories when I talked with him early in development of this book.

"Ask *WHAT*," I replied?

"Whether or not they had to give sex before they could get the abortion," he said. "A very high percentage of women had this happen before abortion was legalized in the U.S. It was quite commonplace."

Dr. Potts is in a position to know. Born and raised in England, he received his medical and PhD degrees from Cambridge and was an advisor on the UK's abortion law before becoming the first medical director of the International Planned Parenthood Federation in 1968. After becoming the first physician to promote use of the "uterine manual vacuum aspiration" technique in the early 1970s he moved to the U.S. In the years since, he has produced a long list of books and papers, served as CEO of Family Health International and, since 1993, held an endowed chair in Population and Family Planning at the University of California, Berkeley. When I first began asking around for abortion stories, the most frequent response I got was, "Have you talked with Malcolm Potts?" But I was taken aback by his question.

"Okay," I said, "I'll ask."

When the storytellers I spoke with after that were asked, only one answered in the affirmative. She offered only the sketchiest details and did not want her story retold. "I do believe it happened fairly often, though," she said. "We were utterly vulnerable and powerless, and bad men went into the abortion business. For myself, I can only say that nothing in my life before or since has been as terrible. I don't think anyone needs to hear the details. People just need to know that when you are already suffering and in pain, to have something like that happen to you changes you forever. You are either destroyed, or you somehow manage to climb back into humanity." She is now a minister in an East Coast church.

A few women, while not having "had to give sex," were molested by their abortionists, and these men belong in the Truly Evil category with the others.

Pat Forman was a 19-year-old junior in college when she discovered she was pregnant. "I had never known anyone who got pregnant," she says, "except for one girl. She was sent away to a coal mining town where she gave up the baby. She sent me one postcard saying she was locked up. I have no idea what eventually happened to her."

Pat and her boyfriend, who would later become her husband, had both worked for a psychologist who ran a program for children. "He was a good friend, and very protective of us," she recalls. They appealed to him for help, and were referred to an Ob/Gyn in New York City who would perform a safe procedure. *"For $3,000,"* Pat says. "This was 1971. We were college students." They managed to scrape up the money—with a little help from a friend who ran a bookmaking operation—but it took her boyfriend several years of working nights and weekends to pay off the debt.

They went to a clinic in New York, a small, private doctors' hospital. "The doctor drew blood from my boyfriend's arm, injected it into my vagina and all over me, and then said, 'I'm calling in to say this woman needs an immediate D&C.' He said, *Do not let anyone examine you.*" Pat took those instructions as seriously as they were delivered; she recalls being thoroughly terrified throughout. While her boyfriend went to the business office to settle the bill and she was left waiting, a hospital resident came into her room. "I screamed, *'don't touch me!'* and I think I scared him to death too. But he left the room without a word." Finally ready for the procedure, Pat was slipping out of consciousness when she became aware of the doctor's hands "all over my body, while he's saying 'I'm going to make it all right.'" At some point he invited her out on a date. She declined. After coming out from under the anesthesia, Pat did wind up going out on a date—with her boyfriend on the night of her abortion. It was New Year's Eve.

Pat adds a postscript to her tale. "When I moved to New York City in 1972, happily pregnant with my now grown daughter, I began to look for a Lamaze doctor. There weren't that many back then. But I got a list somewhere, and guess who was on it? That creepy doctor who did my abortion. It sickened me to realize that this guy was in such a position. He had no morals; he just went where the money was. His name was at the top of the list."

Another *'Can you believe this?'* story was told by a woman who had an abortion in Ohio in the mid-1960s.

"I had finished my first semester in nursing school," she says, "and was home for the summer, in a small town not far from Cincinnati. My boyfriend, whom I married six years later, was in medical school at the time. He found someone through a friend of his, called to set things up, and went with me to where we were told to meet. They told my boyfriend he could not come with me, and we figured that was standard procedure—and probably okay. At any rate, we had no choice.

"A fairly nice looking, older man drove up in the car we'd been told to look for, and I got in alone. Was I handed a blindfold? No. But he did drive pretty fast, going around blocks in a way that seemed intended to keep me confused. We did not talk. I was somewhat relieved to see a woman at the house where we finally arrived, after driving around for about 30 minutes. It was an ordinary-looking, two-story house in a suburban area that looked sort of run-down. The woman took me to a back room on the ground floor, where there was a bed with stirrups. It was also somehow encouraging to see that the room was clean and apparently set up for what they were doing.

"After I got up on the bed the woman left the room, and immediately another man came in. I was horrified to realize that I knew who he was. Not as an acquaintance, or even by name, but I recognized him as a man who worked in a store where I had had a summer job the year before, between high school and nursing school. At that point, every ounce of confidence and assurance I had conjured up vanished. I figured he would recognize me, and terrible things would happen. The way, in the movies, the bad guy realizes he has been recognized so he has to wipe out the innocent victim. My heart was beating a mile a minute. All I could think of was that I knew I could get his name and address if I wanted, and he would know that. I was as scared as I've ever been in my life. I very quickly put my arm across my face and turned my head. My legs were in the stirrups and there was absolutely nothing I could have done.

"He never spoke but a couple of sentences. It was over in a matter of minutes, and he left the room. When the woman came back in with a packet of supplies and pills, I was in tears. I suppose she had seen a lot of young women get tearful. She patted me on the shoulder, handed me a tissue and said everything would be fine, not to worry. Then she led me back to the side door where the same car was waiting with the same driver. As we headed back to where my boyfriend was waiting, little by little I began to breathe again. All I can imagine is that he did not, in fact, recognize me. But the terrors I felt over the scenarios I dreamed up in those few minutes were worse than any I've had before or since. I avoided that store for the rest of the time we lived in the Cincinnati area. I later had three healthy children, who never heard this story."

Like some others who shared their stories, the woman above felt no animosity toward any of the three conspirators in her frightening experience. "I don't think they were particularly bad, though they surely were in a business they shouldn't have been in: they were breaking the law and were in it strictly for the money. My husband—my boyfriend at the time—never told any of his friends I had recognized the guy, for obvious reasons. But you know? I think they were just ordinary people."

Somewhere in between the good doctors who believed women have the right to the full range of excellent reproductive care—abortion providers who took great risks when it was illegal and who today fight to preserve access—and the bad characters who left death and damage in their wake, were the rest of the abortionists of pre-Roe days. One such in-between was Dr. Benedict Kudish. Pam Lowry, whose story of being blackmailed is told in Chapter Two, found Dr. Kudish through a woman who had gone to him for an abortion. Until the operation was uncovered, Lowry fielded calls at her apartment and directed women to him.

"He was a general surgeon," Lowry recalls, "with a small office in Brighton less than a mile from St. Mary's Hospital. It was a legitimate medical practice. But apparently at some point he had run afoul of the medical profession over an insurance claim. He was annoyed with the system, and my guess is that doing illegal abortions was one of his ways to get back."

Kudish was a short man, "eastern European looking with gray, grizzled hair, a peasant build, gravelly voice and wry sense of humor," Lowry says. "He spoke about how he thought that if abortion became legal he should write a book about his experiences and he would title it 'The Pillow Always Falls to the Left.'" The book title derived from the fact that Kudish used trilene gas for anesthesia, with one nurse assistant at his right. When the gas took effect, the patient would drop the mask—invariably to the side away from the assistant. "He told the story with a twinkle in his eye," Lowry recalls.

Kudish "was pleased to provide safe abortions," Lowry says, "but it was in no way done for a 'cause.' It amused him enormously that I was giving my time (taking phone calls, giving out information) for free. His prices were modest; he was not part of any vast network or mafia thing; but he wouldn't have done it for free." Lowry remembers one other interesting detail about Kudish, "a minor thing, but it spoke to his personal pride." It seems Kudish had perfected a technique for the ultimate tonsillectomy. He had taught himself to be ambidextrous, working bi-handed to achieve "a completely even cut." Lowry and I opted not to imagine any parallels between Kudish's abortion and tonsillectomy techniques. In the collaboration they maintained for a number of months, no woman Lowry sent to Kudish for an abortion ever reported having a problem. But he was, in fact, committing a crime with every procedure. He also may not have been as expert as he professed to be. After their operation was exposed he was arrested "for complicity in an abortion ring with an extensive practice;" and at his subsequent trial a woman testified that he was indeed the abortionist who left her with a perforated uterus. Kudish avoided going to jail by resigning from the practice of medicine; later attempts to have his license restored were denied.

Florence, who tells her family story in Chapter Nine, offers one of the rare glimpses of a woman abortionist operating illegally before 1973, and one of the few stories from African American communities developed while collecting material for this book. Now retired from a long career in the healthcare field, Florence is also the only person I know who claims her abortionist as a role model.

"She was a saint. Because ours was such a close-knit, deeply religious community, and abortion absolutely out of the question, when I was unfortunately pregnant I thought I had no choice but to drop out of school and have the baby. But when I confided in a trusted, older relative she took me to her friend, 'Aunt Mae.' I don't think Aunt Mae ran any sort of abortion business, but it was clear she knew what she was doing. She told me she had worked in a hospital. 'I was just a cleaning lady, I couldn't have been a nurse,' she said. 'But in those days there weren't so many rules and I did my share of learning.' She was round like Mrs. Santa Claus, black like me; her hair was snow white, her smile was permanent. I have never known anyone more compassionate in my life, or anyone more committed to helping me through a bad time that could have ruined my life—just as it could have ruined her own by landing her in jail. If anything had gone wrong, and I had wound up in the hospital, she had to have known how easy it would be for her to be found and arrested. Everything went fine. I had the abortion early in the morning, spent the day in bed at her house being cared for like a wounded child—which I was—and fussed over by Aunt Mae. In all the years I have worked in healthcare I have tried to be just like her."

Illegal abortionists came in all shapes and sizes, races and genders, from saint to sinner. When Florence was sharing her story I told her about other stories in this chapter. "If we do indeed return to a situation here in the U.S. that compares with the situation in Kenya," she said, "I only hope there will be some Aunt Maes still available."

One other physician offered insight into who the illegal abortionists were. He is a now-retired family practice doctor who spent his professional life in a small, middle-American city. "I was one of those," he says. "I think there were a good number of us, especially in the late 1950s and '60s as we moved toward passage of Roe v. Wade. We were not quite like those you have described except perhaps the Ob-Gyn in Pennsylvania who sought to help a particular population of women. I have no idea who he was or if he accepted payment.

"Fresh out of medical school in a major metropolitan city, I joined forces with five or six other like-minded young men. We were energetic and idealistic. We knew we were taking a big risk, but none of us thought seriously about the price we would pay if we were caught; we just did not think about getting caught. We were absolutely focused on the plight of young women who were desperate to end unwanted pregnancies and had nowhere to turn—there were a *lot* of them. We felt morally obligated to help them. We were also focused on women's health and believed this was part of it. At least two of the men I was closest to went on to specialize in Ob-Gyn.

"We were connected to a small clinic where we could see patients and perform safe procedures, many of which were recorded as appendectomies. We also worked in the apartment of one of the men, in circumstances that were never reported. If I remember right, a few sympathetic doctors in the nearby municipal hospital occasionally did abortions there and recorded them as appendectomies or D&Cs; I can't verify that, though. What I do know is that we had a steady stream of women—sometimes 6 or 8 in a week—guided to us mainly from clergy members. In every single one of these instances we believed—and I think correctly—that we were working within the highest medical and ethical standards, providing the best care we could to women who needed it. We never took payment of any kind. Sometimes we had very affluent women come in who were insistent on paying something. Early on, we set up a fund that could be used when very poor women needed something like child care or other help."

This former lawbreaker says he never discussed their clandestine operation with anyone other than his fellow newly-minted physicians. "I was involved with it for a little more than a year. I think it was going on before I joined with the others, and continued after I left. But I married and moved to the city where I still live. There was never any cause to talk about what I'd done earlier. And happily, Roe v. Wade soon passed. Had it not, I think I would have found a way to provide abortions for women in my care who needed them. But it was a very different world then."

Almost everyone who contributed stories and comments for this chapter expressed concern about the fate of disempowered women if abortion becomes widely unavailable in the U.S. A few "Aunt Maes" and compassionate physicians willing to take risks could be good news for such women, but the risks might well be even greater than a half-century ago.

# Chapter Four

# Leaving, On a Jet Plane

Mandy's story, which happened in 2009, suggests that the gap between haves and have-nots still works to limit women's choices. "We couldn't come up with the money," Mandy told me one recent, sunny afternoon. Her voice was thin and tired. With her permission, an abortion provider in one of the states where abortion is heavily restricted had given me Mandy's name and phone number. She answered on the first ring.

"It got to where I was too far along by the time I might have gotten it done. If my boyfriend and I had been able to raise the plane fare everything would've been OK. But it was a lot of money and neither of us had anything to spare. I have a waitress job that doesn't pay much and I'd had to miss a lot with my first baby being sick. We thought about driving but it would've taken too many days and it would also have cost too much money. My boyfriend works construction jobs. He hadn't found much work." Mandy's words came in bursts, with pauses for breath as if it were hard to keep going.

Mandy had tried to self-abort. It didn't work, but she managed not to do herself serious harm, and the baby was born prematurely. She wound up with two babies under two years old, both with serious health problems, neither likely to get much in the way of care and attention, according to the doctor. Mandy says she will do her best to raise the babies and not to get pregnant again. "My boyfriend, he doesn't know much about raising kids. If we could've come up with the money to get to where there's a clinic, we'd have been a lot better off, all of us." Other than those brief remarks, Mandy was not interested in talking about her experiences or her life. From what I was able to learn, though, that sad remark, "we'd have been a lot better off, all of us," seemed an understatement.

The doctor who connected me with her said Mandy was frail and subject to depression. "I tried to get her decent prenatal care when we realized she could not access an abortion clinic until too late. I'm afraid, though, that this new baby is going to have a difficult life, and make life a lot harder for the whole family. She and her boyfriend are both just 19 years old. In another five or ten years they might be better prepared to have children." The doctor had no long-term relationship with Mandy, but she spoke of the case as one that saddened her because access to an abortion when she first sought it would have prevented what looks like years of hardship ahead.

Another young woman I talked with who is a few years older than Mandy had a much happier story. She had gotten pregnant by a man she did not love and had not seen since their brief period of intimacy. She had a good job but was still in graduate school with no interest in being a mother at this time. She also said she did not "have the skill set for" motherhood. Because she did not have a private physician, an option lay in the clinic nearby which offered abortions. But she would have had to make at least several trips, and dealing with the surrounding protesters seemed unpleasant and a little scary. So she gave herself a weekend trip to New York, including a Broadway show and an abortion. The cost: one round-trip plane fare, two nights in a hotel, clinic fees—and orchestra seats for herself and a friend at the show. "But was it worth it? You bet. Ten years from now when I am ready for a child I think it will seem even more worth it."

For those with reasonable resources who live in states where multiple restrictions or scary protesters make local abortion difficult, travel to a friendlier state is not much of a problem; for others, like Mandy, it can be impossible.

Leaving the country was the first best option—if one could afford it—for having a safe abortion before it was legal in the U.S. For the most part those who went to Japan, Switzerland, London or Canada found themselves in good hands; Mexico was a mixed bag. Excellent options were occasionally found in other European or Asian cities, especially for women who had friends or relatives to help make arrangements.

In 1968, five years before Roe v. Wade would change the land-scape of women's rights in the U.S., the political focus was on an-other country: Vietnam. An increasingly unpopular war was about to become Lyndon Johnson's war; it was already the primary issue splitting the country in a tumultuous decade. Phyllis, a young high school student in Seattle, was caught up in politics and protest with an intensity that would propel her eventually into a long and dis-tinguished career in law. Today Phyllis is a tall, strikingly attractive woman who exudes competence and authority. It is easy to picture her as a very pretty teenager; but she was more than a pretty face. "What happened in those early months of 1968, my senior year in high school, was the turning point of my life," she says. "Watching on TV the eloquent speeches of Martin Luther King, and then his assas-sination, the shooting of a Viet Cong prisoner by a South Vietnamese officer, the assassination of Robert Kennedy—absolutely galvanized my friends and me. We were out working precincts, joining protest marches, handing out flyers on street corners. The turmoil of those days was absolutely beyond imagination. Getting pregnant was just as unimaginable."

Phyllis had never been out of her home state of Washington. "De-spite my emerging activism, I had what you could call a 'protected' upbringing. It included excursions to nearby parks with the family, but that's about as far afield as I had ever traveled. Going to Japan? I wanted to go to Washington D.C."

Japan was the destination of choice recommended by Phyllis' fam-ily physician when she told him she would have to have an abortion, and asked for his help. Phyllis had been impregnated by a man who was twenty years her senior, a recent widower who had long been a friend of her parents. She had felt sorry for him, "and at the time—which was a very different time from today—I also felt somehow to blame for everything. The whole country was exploding, my parents were distraught about losing one of their best friends, it was easy to be overly friendly while doing my part to ease the grief of a recent widower." When she told them of her pregnancy, in the summer of 1968, Phyllis felt that her parents and the widower all three reacted more with dismay about its potential social implications than anything else. "Looking back all these years later, I think my parents felt that their friend the widower had simply 'forgotten himself' in his grief. They had been so filled with grief themselves—he and his wife had both been in their wedding and his wife was still in her forties when she died—they didn't focus much on me. I absolutely *hated* telling my parents. It felt demeaning, and embarrassing, and took three or four sleepless nights before I could gather up the courage to do it. And then they seemed hardly worried about me and not particuarly angry with him. Actually, I wasn't all that angry with him myself; I just knew I could not continue with the pregnancy.

"My parents were fully supportive of my having an abortion. I did not love this man, although I'd been caught up in the drama of it all and was certainly infatuated with him. I was in no way prepared to raise a child, and I had already mapped out the college and career choices that were to begin in the fall. I had gone first to our family doctor, who confirmed the pregnancy and told me about the place he knew in Japan. Then I screwed up my courage and told my parents. I think they bought the plane ticket that afternoon."

Phyllis' only problem en route—she went alone—was being sick on the plane. "My father had bought a first class ticket for me, though," she says, "and I was fussed over something ridiculous by the crew. They thought I was just young and nervous about being on my first flight. I told the flight attendant I was going to visit a friend. Of course I *was* young and nervous. And frightened, because I didn't know what would happen. I couldn't understand why I had to go to these extremes of trouble and expense—even if it was my father's expense—for something our family physician could have taken care of in an afternoon."

The plane was met by a couple who seemed to be in their mid-forties, both of whom spoke perfect English. "They drove me to a hotel, handed me a sheet of instructions and information, and told me they would pick me up at eight AM the next morning. I had dinner at the hotel. Mostly plain rice, while reading about anesthesia. It is not the way you want to build memories of a new country."

Everything went without incident. "The clinic was spotless and almost everyone there also spoke English," Phyllis says. "I was back on the plane home the next day. I've done a good bit of traveling in my adult life, but oddly enough I've never gotten back to Japan. There may be something psychic going on with that."

The two women I spoke with for this book who had abortions in Switzerland tell of experiences almost as unremarkable as Phyllis' international round trip. "I flew from New York to Geneva," said one. "I signed a paper in the doctor's office, had the procedure and flew home the next day. There's really nothing to add—except that it makes me furious now to see my grandchildren's right to choose disappearing. Because my family had money I was able to have a safe procedure and get on with my life; what about the women today who are poor, and have no one to stand up for them?"

My very good friend Liz Campbell tells a similar, long-ago-in-Switzerland story. But Liz' story is worth repeating for the other counterpoints it draws, particularly with powerhouse African American activist Loretta Ross, whose own story is told in chapter X. The two are close in age and similar in their ferocious passion for justice.

Liz is the daughter and only child of famed African American cartoonist/illustrator E. Simms Campbell (1906-1971) whose work appeared in slick magazines for several decades and who created, among other notable characters, Esquire Magazine's mustachioed "Esky" mascot. She grew up in Westchester County, New York and Switzerland, in homes that would have seemed posh to the young Loretta. The Campbells frequently hosted African American artists, writers and leaders, some of them prominent in the fight for justice. They got scant notice from Liz. About those visitors, and the turbulent times of the civil rights movement in the U.S., she says, "I was just too busy being Elizabeth Ann." Reproductive rights for young women would not have been high on her father's list of social justice issues. Pregnant at 18, she went with her mother—"my father would have killed me"—to a doctor's office in Zurich. "You had to sign a paper saying the abortion was necessary for medical reasons, which could include mental health, that was all." An artist herself, Liz Campbell did not grow up focusing on activism. But like Loretta Ross she became a mother, grandmother and fierce believer in women's rights.

For women on the west coast, with or without a lot of money, Mexico was a more common destination. There were places to go for relatively safe abortions south of the border—and others that were decidedly unsafe. A young activist in the San Francisco Bay area named Patricia Maginnis, after agitating for five years for legal abortion, finally opted to take matters into her own hands. In June, 1966, Maginnis started passing out leaflets with names of physicians in both Mexico and Japan who would perform abortions. Her informal, underground and decidedly illegal referral service soon mushroomed into a large-scale operation with a steadily growing clientele.

One young woman who found help by finding Maginnis' network was my husband's niece Betty Barker. "I don't remember how, exactly," she says now. "Everybody just knew to call Patricia Maginnis."

Betty was 17 and more than a little frightened when she realized she was pregnant. "I was very lucky to find out about Patricia via the *Berkeley Barb*," she says. "Patricia herself had gotten pregnant three times using three different types of birth control, and she was trying to repeal all anti-abortion laws. She gave us information and names of doctors willing to perform abortions in safe conditions. In return, we had to be activists, and write to the appropriate elected officials about our wish to have abortion laws repealed." Maginnis also instructed the women that if anything went wrong afterward they were to go immediately to a hospital.

When she began her search for help, Betty was amused to discover that different doctors had different fees, but "you could get a student discount, and another discount if you said Patricia had recommended them." Once she had settled on a willing doctor, Betty recalls, everything changed. "It was all very cloak and dagger, meeting people in a parking lot and then being transported in a van so we didn't know where we were being taken. It was supposed to be in Mexico, but I believe we met them in San Diego."

Though dangerous and illegal, Betty looks back on her overall experience as better than many. It included moments of comfort and support, and her high school sweetheart boyfriend accompanied her—on a trip financed by his mother "as a Disneyland vacation. The doctor who did the procedure used ether, in a bedroom of a nice house that had been converted into a makeshift surgical suite. I can remember waking up before it was over, and someone was holding my hand and comforting me. I thought that it had just started and requested more ether. It was a lot to handle at 17, but I was lucky not to have gone to a butcher." Betty's lasting regret is having had to lie to her own mother and having taken so much money, though it was willingly given, from her boyfriend's mother. "She was a very hard working janitor at Kaiser Hospital, a wonderful, loving woman who had emigrated from Latvia to make a good life for her sons." The vacation did happen. Betty remembers feeling fine the next morning, grateful for having found a sympathetic doctor to perform her abortion. And the next morning the two teenagers went to Disneyland.

Betty and her boyfriend were far luckier than Sara. Sara just remembers that "a friend of a friend of a friend" suggested the clinic she went to in Mexico, and she has regretted that adventure ever since. "I was young and naïve and alone and terrified," she says. "I was so glad to have a contact number, and to believe the whole mess would be over, it was as if I were on auto-pilot. If anyone had suggested I might be in danger—which no one did, mainly because just about no one knew—it probably wouldn't have stopped me."

Sara was a victim of date rape "before they invented the term." They were both in their late teens, students at a major western university and part of a large, loose-knit group of friends. Her boyfriend was popular, "lots more popular than I was." His raping her had led to a bitter fight, after which she told him she never wanted to see him again. "I really couldn't avoid seeing him," she says, "but I stayed as far away as I could and I never spoke to him again. If I had known right off that I was also pregnant—well, there was no way I could have been any more humiliated and angry."

For weeks Sara tried denial. She says the idea of complaining to campus or local police was out of the question, "and if I went to a hospital I would still have had to 'prove' I had been raped. In those days it would have been my word against his and resulted in a whole lot of ugliness. I'm not sure it's much different today." Eventually Sara went to a doctor in a nearby town who confirmed the pregnancy. He "seemed terribly disapproving" and suggested a place she could go to have the baby and put it up for adoption. "Can you imagine what that felt like to me?"

Instead, Sara began cautiously asking around. "I was terrified that word might get out that I was pregnant," she says. "Not only would it have been hard on me and my family, I felt it somehow tied me to that boy." After a few discreet questions, one friend came up with the number of a place in Tijuana where she might go for an abortion. "Much later," Sara says, "I heard all those rumors and horror stories about Tijuana abortions, but at the time I hardly even knew the city existed. I just knew it was close enough to drive in one day. So I borrowed the family car, told my parents I was meeting some friends for a weekend at the beach and left early one Friday morning. After I crossed the border I called the number again and went to the place where they told me I'd be met. I left the car at my hotel. I got in the taxi with a man who spoke very broken English—I spoke no Spanish at all—and we drove to an area of the city that looked really bad. I wanted to call the whole thing off, but didn't know what I could do next. I was taken into a small house. There were three men there. First, they told me the price had gone up and they wanted $400, not the $300 I had been told. I had about $350 on me. I said they could have it all, just do the abortion and get me back to the hotel. I was then raped by one of the men. I think I passed out. I hardly remember what happened, except I heard one of the other men say to me, 'We finish now.' and I thought I was going to die. All alone, in some godforsaken Mexican city where I would never be found." Instead, a very crude abortion was done and Sara was delivered back to her hotel.

"I immediately checked out of the hotel, got in the car, drove back across the border and straight to the emergency room of a hospital in San Diego. That was the first smart thing I had done in weeks. They admitted me, and started treatment for infection and God knows what else. The people at the hospital were very kind but they asked a lot of questions I did not want to answer. It was obvious I was the victim of a botched abortion. The police did come and question me, but since this had happened in Tijuana—I told them only that I had been raped there, although we all knew I'd gone there for an abortion. I didn't want to try to do anything about it, they said they wouldn't pursue the matter. I was of course out of money now too, but lucky that I had a checkbook and a small savings account that I raided when I got back home." Sara finished up that year, transferred to another university and left school to get married after her junior year. She never told her parents, her husband or any of her friends until decades later, when she began to work as a volunteer for Planned Parenthood. Though she had several pregnancies that ended early, she was never able to have children.

The delays encountered in the search for a safe abortion outside the U.S.—finding the clinic, raising the money, getting the visa—often led to procedures far more dangerous than they would have been weeks earlier. Denise's mid-1960s pregnancy also ended with a trip to Mexico, but only after attempts to get to other countries were unsuccessful. For women like Denise, it was a harrowing search while the clock kept ticking.

Denise arrived in New York for a teaching job several years before abortion was legalized in the state, fresh out of graduate school at the University of California at Berkeley. Though it was a heady and happy time, she was too busy getting started on her career to cultivate many new friendships. In her second year on the job she attended an education conference where she met and fell in love with Jim. He was bright and attractive and everything she admired. It was only after she became pregnant that Denise discovered he was also married. A frantic, cross-country saga of multiple attempts to end the pregnancy began. First was getting confirmation of the pregnancy. "That took an interminable wait of a week or ten days, because the rabbit had to die or something," she says. Then there were follow-ups on leads to possible safe abortions in Canada and London. But her closest friends—those who might really be able to help—were on the west coast, a long way away in the days before e-mail and inexpensive long distance phone calls. And the leads went nowhere. As the days and weeks went by, Denise tried not to panic.

"My periods had always been irregular," Denise says, "so I didn't really know how far along I was. Jim wanted nothing to do with it. The fact that I was still new to New York was pertinent, because I did not have a circle of close friends; I also didn't have any money. I contacted one woman I did know, and her husband put me in touch with someone in Pennsylvania who was doing abortions…but by the time I was able to make that contact it did not work out. And time keeps going by.

"By then I was probably in my third month. Next, I managed to find someone in New Jersey, went there and was semi-molested." While she was not explicitly asked for sex, Denise says the New Jersey abortionist made suggestive comments and frightening, inappropriate moves. "I managed to get out of there and back to New York in one piece."

Increasingly panicky, still working hard at her teaching job and not feeling well at all, Denise called Hazel, a college friend in California.

"Hazel had a friend who said she could find me a place in Mexico, where abortion was legal," Denise says, "and they would be willing to take me there. We would go across the border from Yuma, AZ to Mexico. I would need $50 in cash—plus the plane fare to Yuma and back. I also paid for their gas to drive to Yuma." The clock kept right on ticking.

Denise bought a fake wedding ring, believing she would need to be married in order to have the abortion. She remembers she was wearing one of the A-line tent dresses popular at the time, and had her money stashed in a change purse tucked into her nylon stockings. With her debts piling up, taking off from work was impossible. Denise traveled through multiple flight changes to meet her friends in Yuma; they spent the night at a cheap motel there and drove to a clinic just over the border the following morning.

"When it was over, I really didn't feel well," Denise recalls; "but I only had one day to travel each way because I had to get back to work. On the way back to Yuma I remember taking off the ring and throwing it into the desert."

Although the abortion itself went without problems, the trip home and days thereafter were filled with pain and sadness. "I remember just wanting so desperately to go home and have my parents take care of me. I managed to get on the plane to New York and back to my apartment, but by then I had a raging fever and was bleeding heavily. I called a friend from U.C.Berkeley who was among the few people I knew pretty well in New York. He came over, and I finally told him. I didn't think I could go to the hospital because I'd be arrested. He brought me some antibiotics, and eventually the fever went down."

Denise tried to have children in later years but always suffered a miscarriage. She notes a final irony as a postscript to her story. "When I moved into the building where I still live," she says, "I discovered that Jim was living there with his wife and family." A half century after this episode I was introduced to Denise by our mutual friend Hazel, who still lives in California but enjoys adventure travel to Europe, Asia and elsewhere. "If only," she remarked, while thinking back on those frantic days, "we'd had such easy air travel when she needed it. If only we'd had legal abortion."

For many of the more fortunate American women seeking an abortion before 1973, especially those living on the east coast, London was the destination of choice. It was a long flight and necessitated at least one or two nights out of the country—which had finally made it impossible for Denise. But there was no language barrier and women could be assured of excellent care. My friend Jacqueline Thompson, a British expatriate now living in San Francisco where she maintains a home and a business as a ceramic artist, offers a view of what services women could find in those years.

"My sister had had an abortion in the counties (that's British for 'not exactly rural, more like the outer edges of New Jersey as opposed to New York City') during the 1960s," Jacqueline says, "and the doctor had to give a note saying it was 'in the interest of the mother's health.' This was probably 1967 or '68. Things changed quite a bit from the 1960s to the 70s, though. When I had an abortion in the mid-1970s, I just popped right into the Marie Stopes Clinic, where all good feminists went for pap smears and education about birth control and everything. It was no big deal, and I certainly had no problem at all." Clinic namesake Stopes, Jacqueline added, "was quite a radical. You might want to Google her." A quick internet search reveals that Marie Stopes, (1880-1958) was in a way the British version of Margaret Sanger. A paleobotanist, author and advocate for women's rights, it is she from whom the family planning nongovernmental organization Marie Stopes International gets its name and inspiration.

Marie Stopes clinics today are located across England and in forty other countries, offering sexual and reproductive health services to millions of women and men: pregnancy tests, HIV screenings, vasectomies, abortions and a wide range of other services. Just as Margaret Sanger's primary goal a century ago was and Planned Parenthood's goal is today, Marie Stopes International seeks to prevent unwanted pregnancies. When such pregnancies do happen, these agencies offer counseling and care—and choice of abortion to end the pregnancy. They are housed in facilities that range from the very well-equipped and modern to the bare-bones clinic. Jacqueline's Marie Stopes abortion of three decades ago was in a "very ordinary place, one of those Victorian homes that have been converted to different offices on each floor."

A few years earlier than the experience Jacqueline describes, Barbara had been among the American women to benefit from good British care when such care was not legal in the U.S.. Barbara went from Providence, R.I. to London for an abortion in 1967. "I had a sister who was much older than I," Barbara says, "and she had gone to London for an abortion in 1959 because she had four children well past kindergarten and she and her husband simply did not feel they could handle a new baby. They did not tell their children—I'm quite sure her children still don't know—but she had told me. So I knew immediately to go to her for advice.

"I actually stayed with a friend of theirs in London. I went to the same physician she had seen earlier, it was fast and clean and painless." Whether or not that physician was working at a Marie Stopes clinic remains unknown; Barbara remembers only that she returned to the U.S. un-pregnant and grateful "to be able to have my life back."

In the years before Roe v. Wade made abortion legal in the U.S. similar struggles went on in neighboring Canada—voices of those proclaiming it was wrong pitted against data showing that women were dying needlessly and in large numbers from botched procedures. Things had begun to change by the late 1960s, thanks in large part to the actions of then-Prime Minister Pierre Trudeau who famously remarked, "The state has no business in the bedrooms of the nation." Change was also coming in the U.S., with developments like New York's legalization of the procedure in 1970. But for women in northern areas of adjacent states such as Illinois and Michigan, quick trips across the border for safe procedures were a welcome option.

"We helped a number of women find qualified physicians and excellent care just across the border," says a retired minister who was active in the pro-choice movement shortly before Roe v. Wade was passed. "Because so many of those we helped had very limited means, we were always on the lookout for the least expensive, but still safe, answer. In the late 1960s and early '70s, that was often found in Canada, particularly in big cities like Toronto.

"I remember putting one woman on a Greyhound bus for a two-hour trip across the border. She was very young and very frightened. We managed to get the cash for two tickets so her older sister could go with her, because frankly I didn't think she would be able to follow directions and get where she was supposed to go. It wasn't like we had a vast, international network; we were just a loose-knit group of clergy and volunteers trying to help while staying under the radar. The week after I had sent them off to Canada the older sister walked into my office. 'We had $5 left over,' she said. 'I want you to have it. You saved my sister's life.' Well, that's about all you need to make your whole month."

That minister and every woman whose story is told in these pages would applaud the Marie Stopes vision: "A world in which every birth is wanted," and their mission: "Children by choice, not chance." But many of them worry today that journeys on jet planes or buses could again become a common requirement for women wanting to end unintended pregnancies, and that women unable to afford the travel costs will once again suffer.

# Chapter Five

# Husbands and Lovers

The fear, all these decades later, is palpable.

"What was the worst part of all?" I ask. Without a pause he replies, "Standing on that street corner in the cold, absolutely alone."

This comes from a man who has had a long and distinguished career as a businessman and an activist for good causes, a man few would peg for being so numb with fear on an afternoon half a century ago that it remains lodged in his brain's memory. But as he retells the story the fear is still in his voice.

Barry and Meg (pseudonyms, at his request) were young lovers in New York, busy with families and careers and excited participants in the 1960s cultural revolutions. They would later marry, and have long, happy years together. But in 1967, when they discovered Meg was pregnant, they were each married to someone else. Continuing the pregnancy was, as they saw it, not an option. They actually had one another option, which was to go before a hospital committee and plead mental instability. "I dimly remember knowing of that," he says, "but we could not have gone that route." Barry and Meg both had high profile jobs in Manhattan and pleading mental instability could have wreaked major havoc with her career. They began the search for an abortion, hoping to find a safe procedure outside of New York.

Meg had a college friend in Baltimore through whom they eventually located a doctor in Washington. He would perform the abortion for $600—a daunting sum then despite their both having good jobs. "This was happening right before Thanksgiving," Barry says, "and we had to think of what to tell our families. For her it was no problem; her husband was pretty *laissez-faire* about these things. But my situation was very different, and I had to invent something plausible. I wound up sending myself a telegram saying a former employer had had a heart attack, and I needed to fly to Tampa right away." He flew instead, with Meg, only as far as Washington. They went immediately to the doctor's office near DuPont Circle. "Meg was fearless," he says, "but I was seriously frightened. And I remember waiting for her—I was not allowed to enter the clinic—on the street corner, terrified."

Barry and Meg's story drew to a happy-ending close quite soon. "We had gotten a room at the Jefferson Hotel," he says. "Meg was bleeding quite a bit, but it stopped within a day. So we took the occasion to enjoy the rest of the Thanksgiving weekend on our own."

If Barry was frightened for a few hours, scarier to imagine are all the things that might have gone wrong—and the fact that there would have been no recourse. Meg said the offices were somewhat shabby, but the doctor seemed to be an actual doctor and seemed to have everything he needed. But had any complications arisen, "we could not have gone back. We were given those instructions very explicitly."

Stories without happy endings were everywhere in the days before Roe v. Wade. One was told to me by a colleague recently. We had been at a lunch meeting together, and afterwards were visiting before the room was closed, talking of her projects and of this book. She asked if I were including anything about the "boys" involved, and offered to share one such incident.

"I grew up in a small town outside Chicago," she said, "with two sisters who were considerably older and a brother one year younger. He and I were always exceptionally close. It was one of those working class, close knit, heavily Catholic communities that still exist though I think they're not nearly as happy and carefree as I've always remembered my childhood. My brother John was a year behind me in the public school we went to. We had an experience my senior year in high school I remember as if it were yesterday—and am sure I'll never forget.

"Johnny was a junior. He had a girlfriend, Mary Rose, who was in the same school. Her family lived just a few blocks away and we knew them, but only casually. Mary Rose would sometimes come for dinner when they had been skating or to a ballgame together. I think Johnny had dinner at their house once or twice. As far as I know, Mary Rose's family was fine with Johnny. Of course, nobody had two cars in those days and if they went out on a date they were home early on the bus.

"In the spring of 1971, the year I graduated from high school, Mary Rose suddenly died. She had always been sort of sickly, and the obituary—remember when detailed obituaries always appeared in the local papers?—said that she had been visiting relatives out of town and caught a cold which quickly went to pneumonia. It was a terrible tragedy, but she did have a lot of out-of-town cousins and people did die of pneumonia then, and no eyebrows would have been raised. I remember Johnny going with me to take some food to the family, the thing you did whether you knew them well or not.

"I also remember going to the funeral. It was the first I'd ever been to. I remember Johnny sobbing uncontrollably, which was going on all over the church among the school kids because nobody else had ever had a lot of experience with teenage loss and grief. I felt sad for my brother, but after a few days we had pretty much gone on to other things. Then, probably about ten days after the funeral, Johnny came into my room late one afternoon. My mother was downstairs cooking dinner; it was perfectly normal for him to walk in, sit on the side of the bed and visit. This time he sat on the side of the bed and burst into tears. 'I killed her,' he said; 'I killed her.'

"You did *what*?" I said—not even really sure what he was talking about.

"'Mary Rose,' he said. 'I killed her. A week before she died, she told me she thought she was pregnant. I was scared to death. But I told her I'd do whatever we needed to do. Marry her, if that was the best thing.' Johnny had just turned 18; I think Mary Rose was 17. 'But she said she knew what to do. And that was the last time I spoke to her. I know she couldn't have told anyone. But what did she mean, saying she knew what to do?'

"You have to understand we were such *kids*. I had never had sex, we didn't even talk about it—certainly not with our parents or any adult— and I couldn't imagine my little brother in such a situation. But it had clearly happened, and if Mary Rose hadn't actually been pregnant, she suspected she was. I did the best I could to convince Johnny that he had not caused her death and he mustn't go around blaming himself. I don't know how successful I was.

"My brother went off to college, got married after his sophomore year, had two kids, got divorced when they were in high school, and died of a heart attack in his late forties. We never spoke of Mary Rose again, after that sad, sad conversation in my bedroom with dinner cooking downstairs. I doubt if he ever told another soul. But I have a feeling he never really forgave himself, and when I hear you talking today about your own story, and the stories of other girls desperate to end an unwanted pregnancy, I wonder how many peripheral tragedies there were. How many boys like my poor, good-hearted, guilt-ridden little brother."

There were undoubtedly many. And the dangers facing women and men alike when an unplanned pregnancy pushed them to desperate measures did not magically vanish with the passage of Roe v. Wade. One account of an experience in the days well past 1973 was published anonymously some years ago by Steve Heilig, now a healthcare ethicist and writer based in San Francisco. Heilig offered it for inclusion here, and doesn't mind acknowledging it. Several decades later, the tale of two young lovers has more than a few elements that resonate with young lovers of any age, any era.

"When I was 19 years old", Helig wrote, "I fell crazily in love with a hometown girl. This was very surprising for both of us, as we had been acquainted since childhood, but had never really noticed each other until a certain amount of maturing of mind and body took place. A second surprise, maybe inevitable in retrospect, came along a few months after we began spending virtually every possible hour in each others' arms. She called me from the university she was attending a few hours away and told me she was fairly certain she was pregnant.

"Well, I had thought about this issue in the abstract and we had made some admittedly lackluster attempts at contraception, but here it was for real. We obviously weren't ready for this; we were teenaged undergraduates barely beginning to find out who and what we were, both together and apart. And now there was this big and frightening problem which could not be denied. We could hardly even talk about it, but we tried. She told me she had waited as long as possible before telling me her menstrual period was late, not only out of hope that she was mistaken, but because she was fearful of my reaction. And, yes, I didn't know how to react. So I just asked her what she wanted to do.

"'I have an appointment for a pregnancy test at the health center, and then if it's true, we have to get an abortion,' she said with certainty. Even today, I remember her exact use of the word 'we.' But what she said made sense to me; there was really no question that we were anywhere near ready to become parents. I told her I'd be there whenever and whatever she wanted. I loved her, and even if I didn't, there was no question of walking away, for I felt responsible for her—our—plight.

"The test was positive; her resolve fell to pieces. I drove up to visit her, and we spent a weekend crying together. She became immobilized by some combination of grief and fear, and I frantically took on the responsibility of finding someplace to get an abortion. What I quickly learned was that, even though abortion was legal and she lived in a sophisticated university town with a surplus of doctors and hospitals and even countercultural 'free' clinics, there was no place we could go locally. It seemed no doctor wanted to be singled out as an 'abortionist.' The best they could do, we were told, was to refer us to a clinic in the metropolitan area a couple of hours away. So we made the earliest appointment we could get, two weeks away, and waited.

"The waiting was the worst, at least for me. I felt helpless, watching her fall apart as psychological denial fell away. She said her body began to tell her something was going on. She was strongly maternal even at eighteen years of age, and felt or imagined she felt her body 'humming.' She asked me, a biology student, about embryology and fetal development, and I did some research and told her some of what I learned, although it didn't seem to help her confusion. What was growing inside her was still smaller than a tadpole and similar in shape, I told her. I also learned, and relayed to her, that many very early pregnancies ended spontaneously, and for a while we harbored the feeble hope that we might be saved by nature, but soon there was no denying we would have to take action. She still remained convinced that we were doing the right thing, but that didn't appear to lessen her ambivalence and certainly didn't stop her from feeling frightened and severely conflicted.

"On the appointed day, we drove into the inner city, getting lost on the freeways and then finding the clinic in a seedy area I had never been to before. We were the only Caucasians in the packed waiting room and I was the only male, and I recall wondering 'Where do all the white people go? Where are the men?' I was young and dumb but even then I knew that not only nonwhite people had to deal with this kind of problem. And it seemed strange that none of these women had their men with them, as I was also aware that it was unlikely any of these women had become pregnant alone.

"My lover just sat immobile. By then she had gone into a kind of psychological auto-pilot, and seemed calm when they called her name. I let go of her hand, watched her walk through the door out of the waiting room, and then just sat with all the other women. I listened to a couple of older women mock my clothing and beach sandals, in voices loud enough that I'm sure they knew I could hear them. But I didn't care; to my eye, they had some pretty silly attire on themselves, like pink hair curlers and such. In any event, I had other worries, for it was only while I was waiting alone that paranoia took over and I was sure that something terrible would happen to my beloved. Not only would she be harmed or killed, but everyone would know why, and it would be my fault, and I'd never get over the guilt.

"Of course, she came through it physically unharmed, albeit worn out by all the emotional trauma. I'll never forget the agony of driving home in my old van with her lying in the back, crying tears which I knew I couldn't stop. That trauma would continue for some time as we struggled to figure out what it all meant, if anything. She seemed to react mostly on an emotional level, feeling ill-defined guilt about having had an abortion, about not telling her mother, about our sexual irresponsibility. I tended to feel more analytical, and even though I attempted to share my supposedly rational, hopefully helpful insights with her, it was clear that we were speaking different languages even in the midst of shared love and confusion.

"That itself broadened into a lesson that came to me only over time passed. She and I had shared equally in the genesis of her pregnancy—perhaps me even more so, for, driven by love and hormones and sex roles, I had probably been more aggressive in initiating our sexuality. But the real burden of deciding what to do about the consequences, of feeling the full brunt of our actions and of doing something about it, then fell to her. I made the practical arrangements and paid the fee, but those were things she could and would have taken care of if I weren't around, and I never harbored any illusion that I was carrying even half of the load."

George's story is in many ways the polar opposite. "My first reaction," he says, "was fury. You might call it a male response. She was using an IUD and other contraceptives, and I just immediately thought she had done something wrong. Everything was wrong, at that particular moment of the early 1960s. I had enlisted in the Army right at the end of World War II, and then been called back during the Korean War, which doesn't get much notice but I can tell you it was no picnic. Meanwhile, I'd gotten married. Ten years later I was trying to finish grad school and juggle a low-paying job—and in between all this we had managed to produce four children. Who for some years had an alcoholic father. I remember getting up at an AA meeting and saying, 'My name is George and my wife is pregnant again.' It got a good laugh. At home, we weren't laughing much, even though I was sober.

"This was in North Carolina, where abortion was considered, by most of those we knew, as not only illegal but sinful. We started asking around the university community as quietly as possible, and were able to find a guy we believed to be a doctor. On the appointed day my wife went off, alone, acting as though it was all just fine, and I stayed home with the kids. Our oldest was a teenager by then, a daughter; what my wife had told her about sex in general and abortion in particular was zero. I remember sitting at the kitchen table trying to get some work done, fielding questions from the kids about when Mom would be back, drinking black coffee, wondering if I'd ever see my wife alive again. I didn't even know exactly where she had gone, and I realized that finding her would be next to impossible. It was the longest afternoon of my life.

"She was due back, we thought, by 3:30 or 4:00; she had left home fairly early in the morning to drive to the parking lot where she would meet the abortionist or his driver—we weren't exactly sure which. By 6:00 the kids were getting hungry, she wasn't home and I was more than a little frantic. It was beginning to get dark. I called the casual friend-of-a-friend who had given us the phone number and she tried to reassure me, but all I could think was that I had sent my wife off to die, alone, and would have to live with this knowledge forever. When she walked in the door about 7:30, looking pale but more beautiful than anyone I'd ever seen in my life, I burst into tears."

George and his wife told their kids, in explanation of the emotional scene, that they had had a fight in the morning—a not infrequent occasion in those days—and that he had been afraid she might have left for good. It was a logical explanation for an illogical time. The following week, George had a vasectomy. When his wife died, long before his conversation with me, they had been married for 48 "mostly wonderful" years. They never told their children.

Despite his grateful relief over the way everything worked out, and their lingering anger at the system that denied them the right to choose a safe and legal abortion, neither George nor his wife ever became involved with pro-choice causes. "We just wanted the whole business behind us," he says. "Both of our daughters are married now and have kids of their own, and they will never have to have an unwanted child. At least, I hope not."

The man involved in creating my need for an abortion is now dead and presumably resting in peace, although I think he deserves nothing of the sort. It would be interesting to know what, if any, memories of the time he retained. My guess would be it quickly disappeared from his conscious memory. He is worth mentioning only as an example of the uncounted thousands of men who created unwanted pregnancies and accepted little or no part of the burden. It was, and generally still is, "her problem."

But among the men who were caring and responsible partners when their wives or girlfriends wound up with unwanted pregnancies, lasting memories vary widely. The boyfriend and later husband of one of the women—I'll call her Madeline here to protect his anonymity—who tells her story in an earlier chapter, has been her ex-husband for over a decade. He did not want to be identified, but somewhat reluctantly agreed to share with me his own memories of that time. In a terse long-distance phone conversation he responded to my questions about his perspective:

"That was a very long time ago," he said, "and I haven't really thought much about it since then. I do remember I borrowed the money from a friend, and I worked *every day* for a very long time to pay off the loan." But as for emotional memories—anger, fear, worry, exhaustion—he had none. Just a feeling that could be categorized as satisfaction for having done the right thing. "It was a high class hospital, and the doctor was excellent," he recalls.

Madeline's memories of her time in that hospital are appreciably different. While the hospital was indeed a very good one, the doctor was sexually abusive. Madeline is certain she told her then-boyfriend about the abuse in some detail, but thinks he has probably long forgotten that part of the story for a lot of reasons. She has not. Her abortion was on December 30. The next morning when her boyfriend came to check her out of the hospital, "I was just so glad to see him that I was all smiles. Feeling great. We went out to a New Year's Eve party that night. He told me later that if I had been angry or depressed he would have walked away, feeling he had done his duty, but because I was so upbeat we just picked up where we had left off."

Mark is the long-time husband of a friend of mine who described him as having "what you might call a promiscuous past." He was happy to talk about that past and how it was impacted by illegal abortion.

"Cleveland, Ohio was not that big a town in the late 1950s and early sixties," Mark says. "The friends I still have from those days look back on them, as I do, as sort of a Norman Rockwell childhood. Most of us were from pious Catholic families in which it was taken as law that girls would remain virgins until they married. Most of us boys bragged about sexual adventures we hadn't really had, but the fact was we did fool around a lot with the girls who were reported agreeable. Or with tough girls from tougher neighborhoods. Word got around. It was called sowing wild oats. Occasionally we would have sex with our serious girlfriends—that happened several times with me in my junior and senior years in high school, and those were 'nice girls' which is why I wouldn't want you to use my name. Condom? Never occurred to me. Sex was *never* mentioned in my home, which was solidly middle class. It would have been unthinkable for either of my parents to discuss such a thing with me—God only knows what *they* knew when they got married in 1939—and as long as the family car came home in one piece nobody much cared what had gone on in the back seat.

"I don't know of any girl from that time, or from our social group, who might have had either a do-it-yourself or back alley abortion," Mark says, "but I'm sure it happened because there's no way a lot of those girls didn't get pregnant. I do remember one friend who married quite suddenly during our freshman year in college, and had a baby a rather scandalous seven months later. In high school we also used to talk about how girls would 'trap' you into marriage and you shouldn't believe they're pregnant just because they say so. Thinking about that today it seems terribly cruel, but it was a different culture and a different time. *Everything*'s different today. But I do believe if abortion becomes illegal again women will try the do-it-yourself or the back alley route before they deliver a baby they don't want. At least, an awful lot of them will. Would men today be any more empathetic than I was in my teens and early twenties? I want to think so, but I doubt it."

Arlene Jech, who worked on the ObGyn ward at San Francisco General Hospital remembers her job as filled with terrible stories. "Women would come in with raging fever from blood-borne infections, and we'd just try to stop the bleeding and get their fever down. But we couldn't always do that. They were really scared, and really sick. Usually they had tried to self-abort, using a coathanger. I remember one woman, Hispanic, who died and left six or seven children; she had felt she just couldn't have another baby. Even after the pill was around, women would be caught between what their religion and the culture were telling them, often also what their husbands wanted. It was just so sad. Most of these women were poor, and wanted to know what they could do because they just couldn't see having more children."

Gary's wife might have been on Arlene's ward. "We were both in college," he says, "and not yet married. We had big plans that included having a family five or ten years later. Judy didn't tell me she was pregnant until after she had already tried to self-abort, and was bleeding and sick. We had no money, no insurance, and I took her to the emergency room at SF General late one night, both of us scared to death. After they admitted her I went with her to the ward. It was the worst place I had ever been and that was the worst night of my life." Gary's girlfriend, who soon became his wife, survived, but they were never able to have children. His wife died of breast cancer while still in her forties. "I can't separate either of those facts from the haunting memory of that night at San Francisco General, or the feeling that it was my fault," he says. "I think I'll carry that guilt to my grave."

The late Ralph Stinson, a prominent and widely loved OB/GYN in Northern California, was among the health professionals who for years helped make sure that wanted children came safely into the world. Through providing birth control information and aids such as IUDs, Stinson also helped women avoid having unwanted children. His wife Harriett would eventually found California Republican Women for Choice and become an active supporter of reproductive rights. But in the early years of what would be a long and happy marriage she was a stay-at-home mom with two toddlers barely one year apart in age. Harriett Stinson had a dual problem common to young mothers: the need for a lot of sleep, and the inability to find time for such a luxury. When she was pregnant, though, Harriett's need for a minimum of twelve hours sleep each day became almost pathological. This had not been a critical issue with her second pregnancy, because every time the baby went down for a nap Harriett did too.

When she became pregnant for a third time, the situation was different, and dangerous. If she were suddenly awakened from a nap, for example, she could wake up in a fury. One day, wakened from a sound sleep by her two-year-old son, Harriett went into an uncontrollable rage. She grabbed the child, rushed to a window and reached for the latch so she could hurl him two stories down to the ground below. With one hand and arm encumbered by holding her son, she was fortunately unable to get the window open. Slightly though not thoroughly calmed, she put the child down, closed the door and went back to sleep.

"I was afraid to tell my husband," she recalls, "but I knew I had to. When I did, he was absolutely magnificent. He held me tight, and told me it was common for pregnant women to have their hormones get out of control. 'We're going to do two things,' he said. 'First, we're not going to have the five children we'd wanted; this will be our last child. Second, we're going to hire someone to come in and make sure you get the full 12 hours sleep you need each day.'" It was a compassionate response, and they were able to afford the solution and avoid what might have been a family tragedy.

But Harriett later got pregnant again. She had been using a diaphragm and they had been cautious; but accidental pregnancies still happen. Very early in the pregnancy, before she had even mentioned suspecting it to her husband, a dangerously similar incident occurred. This time it was the same disturbing-the-peace that toddlers invariably will commit, and this time it was a third-story window. "We lived on a hillside," she says, "and the back windows looked out on a concrete area three levels down. When my son woke me from a nap, I went into a rage again, grabbed him and rushed to the window to throw him to the ground. But again, I couldn't manage the locks with one hand so I was prevented from doing what I fully intended to do."

This time her husband was equally sympathetic but considerably more pro-active. "When he came home and I told him, he said, 'we're doing an abortion tonight,' and he performed the abortion then. The next day, when I was awakened from a nap, the chemicals in my body had already receded, and I was able to respond in a normal manner." The Stinson children, spared the consequences of interrupting the nap of a hormonally-crazed mom, all lived to a healthy adulthood.

Harriett Stinson's subsequent activism for women's reproductive rights is probably typical of many women traumatized by unplanned or unwanted pregnancies. In the aftermath of very bad experiences, they wrote papers, studied to be gynecologists or volunteered for reproductive rights organizations; some of their stories are told in the next chapter. The histories of their partners usually went in other directions. Partners tended to get on with careers and family obligations, though remaining sympathetic to women's rights.

One husband who is likely to keep up with abortion rights is a former Marine named Ross Becht. Becht worked as an EMT and paramedic in San Diego (CA) County before going back to school for additional studies in hospital and health care management. His attention was drawn away from the classroom by HR 358, a resolution introduced in the U.S. House of Representatives in October, 2011. The bill would have allowed any hospital or health care provider that receives money from the government, such as Medicare or Medicaid, to refuse to provide abortion services, even if the mother's life were in danger. In an opinion piece published in the San Francisco Chronicle On October 18, 2011, Becht wrote:

> "My wife is eight months pregnant with our first child. We are very lucky because so far it has been pretty easy. My wife reserves the right to disagree, as she was the one with the nausea for the first three months and hasn't been able to lie on her stomach since July. Next month, we are looking forward to going to the hospital, where we'll get to meet our son for the first time.
>
> "Some women, unfortunately, aren't as lucky as we have been. Occasionally, late in the pregnancy, there are complications necessitating an emergency lifesaving abortion. I can't imagine how devastating it would be to be told that my wife's life is in so much danger that my child will have to be aborted. Many pregnant mothers will not have to worry about that psychological trauma much longer because if House Resolution 358 is enacted, they could die instead.

"HR 358 allows any hospital or health care provider that receives money from the government, such as Medicare or Medicaid, to refuse to provide abortion services, even in life-threatening instances. The bill is called officially the Protect Life Act, but appears to actually be a 'two-for-one offer' and is commonly called the Let Women Die bill.

"President Obama's office has already stated that he would veto the bill if it crossed his desk because it 'intrudes on women's reproductive freedom.' The bill's sponsor, Rep. Joseph Pitts (R-PA) will probably cite the subsection that refers to the exemption for 'a life-endangering physical condition caused by or arising from the pregnancy itself.' I worked in emergency medicine for 10 years and don't know any doctor who would refuse to take action and prevent a patient from dying because of his or her personal views.

"However, because HR 358 passed through the House of Representatives on Thursday we are one step closer to allowing, some might say sanctioning, health care providers to forget their duty to act and instead decide whether a pregnant woman can live or die. How much further does one group have to go to attempt to impose their will on another? Some states require a woman to listen to a heartbeat or be forced to look at images from a sonogram. Going for medical help now could be hazardous to your health.

"As a voter, I feel it is absolutely ridiculous that my government would attempt to restrict any potentially lifesaving procedure that is available to a patient.

"As a paramedic, I've seen the crushing blow of the words, 'I'm sorry, your baby is dead.'

"As a husband, my blood turns to ice at the thought of any doctor telling a woman's partner that he or she can't save their wife because they won't perform an abortion."

The "Let Women Die" bill died itself before going to the Senate where it was destined to fail. Ross Becht and his wife welcomed their son into the world in November, 2011. Becht remains haunted by that early, fleeting image of his or someone else's wife left to die because an attending doctor would not perform a lifesaving abortion.

There is no data on images and memories of these sorts carried by husbands and lovers present or past, because the scant data on abortion and reproductive rights doesn't go there. Given the required participation of two adults to create an unwanted pregnancy, though, it is evident that both of them often suffer.

# Chapter Six

# Life, Interrupted

One chilly April afternoon in San Francisco I pulled on my anorak jacket and walked over to the neighborhood shopping center. As I passed the Starbucks on the corner of California and Spruce I noticed a pretty young African American girl standing on the sidewalk in front of the store, dressed in sandals, jeans and a short-sleeved pink tee shirt with "Planned Parenthood" emblazoned across the front. She appeared to be about 15 or 16. She was holding a clip-board with a few papers on it and was there, I presumed, to enlist supporters in the fight against a congressional proposal that would have eliminated funding for the organization. But she was too cold or too shy—mostly the latter, I think—to be having much success. I noticed she smiled at everyone who came her way, but calling attention to herself and her cause was clearly not her strong suit; I didn't notice anyone stopping. So I stopped. "Good for you," I said. "I think de-funding Planned Parenthood is a pretty bad idea." I thought that might prompt a speech, or a request to sign a petition at the least. Instead, she looked at me with soulful eyes and said, "Oh, thank you. Do you know, ma'am? Do you know how much women need help?" In a brief, subsequent conversation I learned that she had, in fact, managed to avoid pregnancy herself with counseling, information and contraceptive help from the organization. It struck me that she was just barely past childhood. I had talked a few days earlier with a woman who had worked for seven years at a Planned Parenthood clinic in Louisiana. "The majority of those I saw were 12, 13, 14 years old," she said. "Mostly I just held their hands."

Set aside everything else that Planned Parenthood does to help women—and earnest young girls willing to stand on a chilly sidewalk for the cause—the provision of abortion services in a few of their clinics is enough to immediately raise the blood pressure of those who oppose a woman's right to choose. Pregnancy testing? Vasectomies? Information on sexually transmitted diseases and how to avoid getting them? Denial of these services does not seem to matter, if only abortion can be denied. But when there was no availability of such services, thousands of girls like my sidewalk friend wound up traumatized, and sometimes dead.

The worst of these stories, in the days before Roe v. Wade, involved young girls with no money or resources, as my sidewalk friend explained was her own case decades later. The 'best' were those that involved young girls who managed to come under the care of a physician and went into the hospital records as an "appendectomy." They were often high school age or younger. But 12 years old? And needing an abortion? Of all the poignant, sad and often startling stories that poured in from friends, and friends of friends, as this book was coming into being, Maureen's was among the most extraordinary.

She sat in my living room, a poised, serenely beautiful woman dressed in casually chic pants, expensive heels and cashmere sweater, her hands resting lightly in her lap. Maureen is a highly educated, successful professional therapist, author and mother. You would not figure her to have grown up with a somewhat clueless mother and a highly abusive father. But having transcended all that, Maureen is rooted in what she has done with her life rather than what life, early on, did to her. Introduced by a mutual friend, she graciously agreed to share the story she has only told to a very few close friends.

"I walked into his anger," she says, of how the incident began. She was 11 years old. Her mother was out for the evening, leaving Maureen in the care of her father, whose dark mood was fueled by alcohol. The way Maureen tells it today sounds as if she were somehow at fault. After she walked into his anger things quickly got worse. Her father's shouts, at what she says was some imagined affront, escalated into a beating, and she suddenly found herself on the floor, being sexually assaulted. When she told her mother, the next day, her mother's response was, "He missed me." When I asked Maureen to explain that she said, "I think it was by way of explaining—as if an 11-year-old could understand something like this—that my father needed sex and my mother happened not to be available right then."

The family was living in New Jersey at the time. Because job opportunities and long-distance moves came swiftly in the mid-20th century, it was not particularly remarkable that Maureen's father took a new job across the country shortly after her nightmare experience. They uprooted within a week, loaded their furniture into a moving van and their personal effects into the family car, and headed west. Maureen had already begun throwing up in the mornings. She remembers being sick every day during the trip, and being told that she probably had appendicitis. Once they reached their destination, a community built almost entirely of newcomers from around the country, Maureen's mother sought out a doctor. "She found a Jewish physician who probably could be counted on to be empathetic to our Jewish family," Maureen says today. Arrangements were immediately made for Maureen to have "an appendectomy." She recalls recovering quickly from the operation, and while she did not question what was removed, she remembers being happy that the morning sickness disappeared, and along with it a persistent depression that had enveloped her like a dark cloud. As an adult, older and wiser, she was able to determine that the scar on her stomach indeed suggested something more than an appendix had been removed. That was confirmed by physicians.

Maureen's chosen field enabled her to work through and beyond the abuse she suffered as a child, but she never forgave her father. "I hated him," she says. "The way I got back at him was by never looking him in the eye. *Never.*" It was her way of denying his existence. Even in those pre-Roe v. Wade days, a child in Maureen's condition would have been granted the right to a safe and legal abortion, had her mother been willing to send her father to prison. But it is hard not to wonder how many child rapes, incestuous or otherwise, led to more dangerous abortions—and how many still take place.

Bev was just a little older than Maureen at the time of her unintended pregnancy, and her teenage hormones were raging. The patient of a therapist friend—who connected us after talking it over with Bev—she now lives in Denver. We were introduced through e-mail, and Bev later shared her story in a phone conversation.

"I was just starting high school," she says. "I was a latch key kid before the term came into popular use. My parents were divorced, my mom worked to pay the bills and my older sister was away at college, so there was no one at home when I got out of school in the afternoon. In the Brooklyn neighborhood where we lived nobody paid a lot of attention to who went into whose apartment during the day, although I was under strict orders never to bring anyone home without immediately telling my mother when I called to check in, and never more than one girl. Of course, kids came all the time, boys and girls both; we just made sure to take the Coke cans to the trash. That was as bad as we got, just hanging out, drinking Coke. But because it was not common for one teenager to be at home all afternoon unsupervised in those days, our apartment was pretty popular. It felt a little daring."

On occasional afternoons Bev would find herself with only one boy on site, "a sort-of boyfriend, you could say." He was two years older and these afternoons, while infrequent, became more and more hormone-driven. "While I did fairly often tell my mother I'd brought home 'a girlfriend', I *never* told her he was there. Eventually one day we wound up having sex. On the living room sofa. It was clumsy and awkward and probably not a lot more fun for him than it was for me. The sofa was one of those awful naugahyde vinyl things popular in homes like mine. I remember thinking mid-passion that we were going to do irreparable and incriminating damage to it—that'll cool your ardor in a hurry, worrying about shoe scuffs and intimate stains on the naugahyde sofa. He somewhat apologetically put his pants back on and left, and that was pretty much the end of that. I saw him in the halls but fortunately he was not in my class. It was as if we were both more embarrassed than anything else, and he never came around after that.

"I was 13. I had only just started having menstrual periods. When I finally figured out I was pregnant it was the most terrifying time of my life. I couldn't go to our family doctor, my sister was too far away to call and I could not even *think* about telling my mother. The school nurse was a terror in her own right, and I knew if I told her she would immediately call my mother and track down the boy involved. I would not have told the boy for a million dollars, and I doubt very much he would have been able to propose a solution. There was a library three blocks from our building, about the only neutral source of information I had,

and I snuck in there a few times looking at books, thinking I could figure out a way to abort. I had never heard of Planned Parenthood, but
of course they couldn't have helped me anyway, if they existed then.

"After about a week of library studies and sleepless nights, I started
trying to self-abort with a knitting needle. Fortunately—since here
I am alive today—I was too timid to do myself real harm. When I
decided I couldn't do it myself, I told an older girl, a senior who had
actually been my babysitter not that long ago. The next day she handed
me a piece of paper with a phone number and the name 'Parker' on it
and said she had been told that this person could "take care of things"
if I could come up with $100. That was more money than my mother
made in a month. But I did have a piggy bank with some babysitter
money of my own, and a few things I could pawn, including some
things like tools I hoped my mother would never miss. I called the
number. A woman answered. I asked to speak to Mr. or Mrs. Parker,
and she said she was Mrs. Parker. I poured out my whole story, praying that she would be sympathetic, and begged for help. I told her I
didn't think I could get $100 but I would bring every penny I could.
Sympathetic she was not. She said, 'You get what you pay for, kid.' That
should have given me a clue."

As she was telling her story I asked Bev about other options, partly
just to interrupt but mainly because decades later it is painful to consider that 'You get what you pay for' comment. Couldn't she at least
have told some older friend? "I was too ashamed. If I'd been older
myself, maybe it would've been different. But shame was what I felt,
shame and fear. Or you could say, panic."

Bev went on with her story. "I left school early the next day, saying
I didn't feel well—which was certainly the truth—and took the bus
to the address 'Mrs. Parker' gave me. I had about $86 in a little green
drawstring bag. The address was an apartment in one of those dingy
buildings on a dingy block I had never been to before although it was
not terribly far from our apartment building. I took the elevator to
the right floor and pushed the doorbell feeling like I was signaling my
doom. But I could not think of *any*thing else to do; I was just frantic
to get this over with. The woman who answered the door was about
40 I guess. She had dark hair with some gray in it, pulled back with
bobby pins. She was wearing a frumpy house dress, an apron and roll-

down stockings but that's about all I remember. What I do remember was my heart sinking when I saw her stern, frowning face and heard her say, 'How much do you have?' I thought she was going to send me away. But instead, she closed the door behind me, took the drawstring bag out of my hand and motioned for me to follow her.

"I remember absolutely nothing else about the time or place, what the apartment looked like, smelled like, anything. She led me into a small, dark bedroom and in a matter of minutes had inserted something into my vagina, given me some pads and told me to go home. She also gave me some pills, and I guess now they were whatever antibiotics were available at the time. I swallowed one as I left and took the others as instructed. They could've been arsenic, I would still have swallowed them. I didn't know whether to feel relieved or just more afraid, but I got home as fast as I possibly could. By that night I was bleeding pretty badly, but miraculously it was tapering off the next day. I had gone on to school, just praying I would quit bleeding, and when it did slow down by the end of the school day I remember experiencing the most overwhelming relief I have ever known, before or since."

In most respects, Bev got off easier than most. The bleeding stopped completely, her periods resumed, she suffered no infection or problems. She never told her mother, her sister, her sometime 'boyfriend' or anyone else, and she remembers almost nothing more about those days. She finished high school, graduated from New York University, married and had a son. But as in so many of the stories recorded here when abuse was involved, the years following her abortion were only a partial ending. The wrap-up would only come years later when she confronted the lingering psychological and emotional damage.

"I have no idea, still, whether that childhood incident has a lot to do with issues I subsequently had regarding intimate relationships," Bev says. "But I know the feelings of fear and isolation, the stark terror that something potentially damaging was being done to my body and the whole tangle of issues—hormonal, psychological, physical—followed me well into my adult life. I have had a *lot* of therapy to sort it all out, all the regular baggage of childhood with that little incident tossed in. A safe abortion, with maybe some counseling thrown in, could've saved me a lot."

The girls in Bev's circumstances who tried with more persistence to self-induce used methods that ranged from old wives tales to often bizarre rumored solutions. They brewed and drank strange potions, tried douches that were often harmful, inserted anything from knitting needles to coat hangers. They almost never sought help from responsible adults. Who may or may not have been able to help anyway.

Norma's story is one of these. In a rambling phone conversation arranged by her sister, an old friend of mine, Norma recalled the experience of her unplanned pregnancy 50 years earlier. She was 15 at the time, she told me, and "head over heels in love" with her high school boyfriend. But the discovery that she was pregnant changed everything.

"This was before the pill, and way before the notion that any responsibility for pregnancy prevention at all rested with the male involved," Norma said. "I don't know if he was even using a condom; I certainly didn't ever ask. But when I told him I was pregnant his response was fury. He said I was trying to ruin his life. *His* life!" Norma lost track of the boyfriend decades ago, but she told me she is still in touch with her inner rage. That much was clear from her voice.

"What that meant was, I was on my own. Mine was a respectable, middle class family in a small town on the Florida coast. There was nobody I could tell, or ask for advice. I couldn't go to our family doctor. There were no public clinics, there was no guidebook for frightened teenagers. I began to try tentative pokings-around and it's a wonder I didn't puncture something and immediately bleed to death.

"Meanwhile I was going to school every day, seeing my former boyfriend in the halls and getting dirty looks from him in the bargain. After about two weeks of this he came up to me one day and wordlessly handed me a slip of folded, lined notebook paper. I can still see that little message. It read, 'My brother says ask this girl,' and it had the name of a girl, with her dormitory room at the University of Florida. No address, no phone number, no nothing; just a name and a dormitory room. Gainesville was a long way away.

"I made up this elaborate story about a science project I was doing that required a trip to talk with some people at the university, and finally sold my mother on the idea that I had to make a trip to Gainesville. I think if my younger brother had not coincidentally been very,

very sick and my mother too distracted to listen carefully it would not have worked. But she gave me the money for a bus ticket and permission for an overnight trip, spending the night with this phantom science major in a phantom dorm. I didn't dare give her the name of the girl or the dorm written on that folded-up paper. Every day at school was worse than the one before. I was feeling sick, and in addition I was sure my boyfriend's brother had told every boy in school that his little brother's dumb girlfriend had gotten herself pregnant. 'Getting yourself pregnant' was actually a casual, pejorative term in fairly frequent use at the time, as if any girl who turned up pregnant had to have gotten that way all by herself."

Norma left very early one Saturday morning for a city she had only seen once or twice and a college campus totally strange to her. Once there, she asked everyone she saw for help in finding the right dorm, telling them she wanted to surprise her sister. It was before the days of locked dormitories. "My knees were literally knocking when I got to the right room," she says; "if she hadn't heard my knock on the door, she would've heard my knees. I was very, very lucky that the right girl was in the right room. I just blurted out that I was pregnant, handed her the note and burst into tears."

From that point on, Norma's story got worse. While not totally unsympathetic, the girl she had sought out had no interest in being a part of Norma's distress. She did, though, reluctantly invite her to come in and sit down. Then she took another piece of paper and wrote down a few words. "This is all I know," she said. "Make up a douche of this and it should work. Please do not ever mention my name to anyone, or come back here. It was very wrong of anybody to give you my name."

On the new scrap of paper were scribbled instructions for a mixture of boric acid and something else Norma says she can't name. "I may not remember correctly what it was, but I think it was pretty dangerous stuff." At the time, she says, she had no idea what the word 'douche' meant. But she went to a nearby drug store, bought the ingredients, got back on the bus and went home. She had somehow thought—"at least I had hoped"—that the college girl would let her spend the night in the dormitory, but it was immediately clear that no such option was open. Telling her mother that she didn't feel well and had decided not to stay overnight, Norma retreated to the bathroom with her purchases. She had spent all the money her mother had given her for meals on boric acid and a douche bag.

By morning Norma was experiencing "the worst cramps I have ever known, before or since," was bleeding heavily and had a raging fever. Her mother took time out from nursing the very sick younger brother to get Norma to the doctor, who immediately had her admitted to the local hospital.

"There was only one bright spot in the entire experience," she says now. "The doctor promised to tell my mother only that I had contracted a 'severe infection.' She was so overwhelmed with caring for *two* seriously ill children she never asked for details. And my father, who was on the road constantly, took a job in another state about a year later, which got me away from the school. I had a pretty awful time in the hospital, but if I remember right I was home within a week. Nobody told me at the time that I would not be able to have children, although this turned out to be the case.

"After I married I did conceive one time, and miscarried at about eight weeks. Because that pregnancy was very complicated and difficult, and the doctor said my uterus was 'too damaged' to risk another, I had a hysterectomy after the miscarriage. We have some wonderful adopted children now. I never told my husband this story, because it just seems too sordid. I did tell my sister, who is eight years older and was living in another state when I was in high school. I told her a few days before my wedding. My little brother eventually recovered from the infectious disease that nearly killed him at the same time I was nearly killing myself. I never told him this story. I don't expect ever to tell anyone else. I hope no one else has to go through anything like that, ever."

Those early encounters that resulted in unintended pregnancies more commonly involved young hormones rather than young love. And often it was neither. It was outright assault, or the carrying-out of a callous plan. Such was the case with Theresa.

A plump, round-faced girl with a sunny smile and strawberry blond curls, Theresa left the family farm in central Virginia to attend a nearby state teacher's college in the fall of 1952. She was the first in her family to go to college. The summer after freshman year, she took a job waiting on tables at a roadside café on Highway #1 to help pay the bills. A man named Frankie took to coming in late for dinner, asking for Theresa's table. After a few nights of big tips and pleasant conversations, he convinced her to join him for a movie. At the drive-in, it was quickly apparent that he was not interested in the movie, and that Theresa was no match for his ardor. Because she was initially accepting of what she thought was just "heavy petting," Theresa says everything happened almost before she realized it. The term "date rape" was not in use at the time. Frankie drove her home, and was never seen again.

Theresa, who had been a virgin before that night, knew within a few weeks that she was pregnant. She begged the family doctor for help, but with no success. Finally, in desperation, she borrowed the family car one morning and went to meet a man whose phone number was given her by another waitress at the café—the only person in whom she had confided other than her doctor. The man took her to an abandoned barn where another man waited with a suitcase. Theresa gave the men all the money she had saved, plus $50 borrowed from her waitress friend. She lay on a makeshift table while something was inserted in her vagina. It was over in minutes. Later, Theresa developed an infection that nearly killed her and left her unable to bear children—but at least alive. It was not until the summer after her junior year that she finished repaying the $50 loan.

Betsy Carpenter's story begins in the young love category, and moves from there into an almost unimaginable—albeit ingenious— solution.

Betsy had just started her sophomore year at Radcliffe College (now part of Harvard University,) was in love with a young Harvard student and "life was rosy," she recalls. One October day in 1949, they went for a bike ride in Concord, where "there was a beautiful field, on a beautiful day, and one thing led to another..." When she missed her menstrual period a few weeks later, Betsy went into a denial that lasted until exam week at Radcliffe at the end of January. During that week she became so exhausted that she wound up at the college health center. She was sent from there to an Ob-Gyn physician who immediately confirmed what she had so desperately tried to wish away.

"We lived in Connecticut," Betsy says, "but my parents had a place in Vermont, and my father was taking the train from New York to meet my mother there that day. I managed to get onto his same train in Boston, and as luck would have it there was an empty seat next to him. So I plopped down, and poured out the whole story. I only saw my father cry twice in my life; that was the first time."

But once the initial shock and considerable tensions abated, Betsy's pragmatic parents began to devise a plan. First option, her father announced, "your mother could go with you to Arizona for your health, you could have the baby and put it up for adoption. Second option: you could marry David, but he has already said he doesn't want to do that. (When she told her boyfriend, Betsy says, he replied that he loved her, but not enough to marry her.) Third, we can find if there's a way to have a safe, legal abortion."

In Connecticut, at the time, one could get a legal abortion if three psychiatrists certified that the mother's mental condition made her unfit to carry the pregnancy to term. As the soundness of Betsy's mind was a little too well known, they didn't think that would work. But in New York, if you had either measles or German measles during the first trimester, a pregnancy could legally be terminated. Betsy's father confided in a physician friend, who came for a visit bearing a vial of German measles culture from his lab, and swabbed Betsy's throat with the germs. She immediately came down with the disease. By the time she was recovered enough she was perilously close to the end of her first trimester, "and I essentially had a Caesarean section." Asked if a case of German measles wasn't a terribly difficult experience at that point, Betsy says that in the grand scheme of things, measles were as nothing.

That was the end of Betsy's pregnancy, but hardly the end of the story. She caught up on her courses at Harvard, but when she presented herself to Radcliffe, "They said, 'You're a fallen woman, and you can't come back.' I then worked for a brief time during the summer doing lab work at Massachusetts General Hospital, and in the fall, with the help of some friends of my parents I got into Cornell." Her Cornell career was soon interrupted by a diagnosis of tuberculosis, which sent her to Trudeau Hospital at Saranac Lake, NY where she met and soon married her first husband, a physician. He told her she must never tell anyone about her abortion, especially anyone in the medical profession, "'because I cannot let my colleagues know.' So when I filled out the form during my first pregnancy of course I said I had never been pregnant. And the obstetrician said, 'Then what's this scar?' I said I had had a cyst."

It was the beginning of a long, conflicted resentment against society in general and the medical profession in particular, despite the fact that after her first husband's death Betsy married yet another distinguished physician with whom she is now happily semi-retired. She has turned her resentment into a fierce advocacy for both reproductive rights and end-of-life choice. It includes an ongoing job as Adjunct Clinical Professor at Stanford University, where she teaches advance care planning to medical students—and encourages her students to know the history of abortion in the U.S. and the implications of a return to criminalizing the procedure.

A more recent story involving youth and loss of innocence came from a Texas healthcare worker I'll call Heather, who was in San Francisco on business and heard about this book project from a mutual friend. She asked that her name and some details be changed. Over coffee at a neighborhood shop Heather poured out her story.

"This was in the early 1980s," she says, "after Roe v. Wade was long in place. So technically I should have been able to get a safe, legal abortion. But I want to share my story because I think stories like it still happen often, and people don't realize that unless clinics like Planned Parenthood—places girls can get counseling and help in addition to an abortion—are more plentiful there is often really no other good option.

"I lived on a farm in the Midwest, close enough to town but nowhere near a metropolitan center or anywhere there was a Planned Parenthood clinic. I rode the school bus to the local high school, where I was a freshman. A boy on the bus, a fairly popular senior, took an interest in me, and of course I was flattered—in spite of the fact that I was pretty confused about my sexual identity. He started saying things like, 'When are you going to turn 16? I have a birthday present for you.' I was not even 15 yet, but didn't want to admit it to this sophisticated senior. One afternoon he told me he would have the family car at school the next day, and if I'd meet him afterwards he'd give me a ride home. So of course I did, and you can see where this is going."

The boy drove off on a side road not far from Heather's farm, drew into a wooded area, pulled her out of the car "laughing, saying he just wanted to show me something interesting, it would only take a minute…It did only take a minute, but it was not interesting. It was shocking, painful, humiliating and scary. He drove me home very fast, explaining that if I told nobody would believe me and he'd see to it I was sorry. He had torn my pants. I was almost immediately more focused on how I would get into the house and up to my room without my mother noticing than on the terrible experience I had just gone through. But I did manage to do that. I got into the tub, later told my mother that I'd fallen down and gotten so muddy I wanted to clean up before coming to talk to her as I usually did first thing when I got home.

"You understand, I had a pretty normal, happy home life and I was very close to my mother—I had two brothers much younger than I— but I think I was like most teenagers in that I would have died before telling my mother. When I soon began to suspect I was pregnant, same thing. It's just not something that's easy to talk about with your mother. And there was nowhere I could go. Nowhere. That's why I feel so strongly now that there should be clinics where young girls can go and get help. Not just for an abortion, but counseling and guidance. If they want to go on with the pregnancy—though I can't imagine any 15-year-old in circumstances like mine who would choose to do so— well, that's fine too. But many of the 'pregnancy counseling clinics' I know of put serious pressure on young girls in this situation to continue the pregnancy, and will not discuss abortion. Young girls need comprehensive care."

Heather told a close friend, another freshman in her school. Together they managed a do-it-yourself abortion which apparently worked and did no permanent harm. Not long after this experience Heather came out to her parents as gay. She and her long-time partner now have a teenage daughter, conceived with donor sperm and carried by the partner. "My partner is strong and healthy and I think we are both great moms. I have no idea if I'd have had any trouble with conception or pregnancy because it was never an issue. In that regard I'm lucky."

After finishing nursing school Heather went into public health work. She has focused on working with teenagers in underserved communities, often guiding young girls to pregnancy counseling and trying hard to focus on prevention. "The reality is," she says, "that hormones rage, sex happens and pregnancies result. If we can teach effectively about contraceptives and healthy habits we can prevent some teen pregnancies, but not all. For those that aren't prevented, the girls need comprehensive care. I am absolutely, positively committed first to reaching out to these children, and second to protecting their reproductive rights."

# Chapter Seven

# Speaking Out

Jackie Speier knows combat. She was not yet 30 years old in 1978 when she went with her boss, then-Congressman Leo J. Ryan, to Jonestown, Guyana in an attempt to rescue constituents from the People's Temple compound. On landing at the airport the group was attacked by supporters of cult leader Jim Jones, leaving Congressman Ryan and six others dead—and Speier, shot five times, lying on the dusty airstrip for 23 hours before help came. Her personal nightmare was followed by the mass murder-suicide of more than 900 Temple followers. Speier survived to plunge into local and state politics, becoming the first California state legislator to give birth while in office and authoring more than 300 bills signed into law by both Republican and Democratic governors. In 2008 she was elected to represent California's 12th Congressional District in the U.S. House of Representatives.

It was there that Speier made headlines in February, 2011 with her spontaneous response to a congressional colleague who trivialized women having had medically necessary second trimester abortions. After a colleague, Rep. Chris Smith (R-NJ) read aloud, during a Republican effort to strip funding from Planned Parenthood, a graphic description of a common second-trimester dilation and evacuation abortion procedure, Speier rose to say that she had had an abortion, at 17 weeks, herself.

"For you to stand on this floor and to suggest, as you have, that somehow this is a procedure that is either welcomed or done cavalierly, or done without any thought, is preposterous." Speier's difficult but necessary decision to terminate a pregnancy had occurred after the fetus had slipped from the uterus to her vagina. She made it clear, then and later, that she had not wanted the abortion and had grieved the loss of her baby. But the message to Rep. Smith—who said of the procedure that the doctor "literally hacks that baby to death"—and the world at large was clear: the decision to have an abortion is difficult, personal and private

Speier says the response was overwhelming. "I gave voice to many women. I even had one colleague come up to me afterwards who hugged me and said, 'You know, I had an abortion. But I could never do that, speak out about it.' For whatever personal reasons, my colleagues on the right have been so effective at hammering away at the procedure as 'murder,' and have twisted and tormented those who have had this very safe, appropriate and legal procedure."

As to the issue of speaking out, Speier has no regrets on her own account, and empathy for those who find it too difficult. "You know," she says, "we are taught from a very early age not to talk about things like our menstrual cycles, etc." But breaking the taboo on such topics is, according to many proponents of women's rights, the only way those rights will be preserved. Breaking the taboo, and reconfirming that control of women's bodies must be left to the women themselves. Or, as the nonprofit Boston Women's Health Book Collective puts it in the organization's more familiar publication and title: *Our Bodies, Ourselves.*

Older women who fight for a woman's right to choose more often than not have an especially strong, personal motivation: a determination to right what seems a very basic wrong—for any woman to be denied control over her own body. And it is likely rooted in an experience or an entire life story so searing that it would be impossible *not* to take up such a battle. "It so shaped who I am," comments one of the outspoken women whose story follows.

Kate Michelman, who served as President of NARAL Pro-Choice America from 1985 to 2004, has been called the face of reproductive rights (*Washington Post*, 1/12/2006) and named one of the capital's 100 most powerful women by *Washingtonian Magazine.* She has never been called timid.

Michelman's interest in women's rights is intensely personal. In the late 1960s she was a Pennsylvania homemaker, married to a college professor. She had put her career in early childhood development on hold to start a family. "I had married my childhood sweetheart at age 20," she writes in a gripping memoir, *With Liberty and Justice for All: A Life Spent Protecting the Right to Choose* (Hudson Street Press, 2005.) "I was a practicing Catholic who accepted the Church's teaching that birth control was a sin. Like many other Catholic wives, I practiced the 'natural' means of contraception—the rhythm method—and believed the claim that breast-feeding prevented pregnancy. I exploded every myth. We had three daughters in three years."

In 1969 her husband walked out on her, and just several weeks later, Michelman learned she was pregnant. She was suddenly in crisis, seeing no way she could have a fourth child while trying to raise the other three single-handedly. She attempted suicide. Then she decided to get an abortion. The stumbling block? She was required by law to have permission from her husband—that same husband who had just abandoned her and their three very young children—in addition to the approval of the hospital's all-male review board. She received both. But Michelman's story of that low point in her life makes it easy to understand the course she took. Helping other women avoid the anguish and humiliation she had endured provided the foundation for a lifelong passion. Eventually she went to work, remarried and became the leading spokeswoman for choice that she still remains.

Recently Michelman has expanded her voice to include economic justice, an issue often tied to reproductive rights. It's also, once again, personal. After a happy second marriage and a period in which she combined simultaneous success in family, business and political activities (she testified at the nomination hearings for Justices Clarence Thomas and Samuel Alito before their appointments to the Supreme Court) Michelman encountered a stretch of misfortune that could defeat the strongest of us. A daughter's horse fell on top of her, leaving her paralyzed and in need of extensive long-term care, and Michelman's beloved husband suffered a long and eventually crippling battle with Parkinson's. The combination of events, and especially the course of her husband's decline and long-term need for round-the-clock care, quickly exhausted her savings and threw the family into debt—despite what had been good incomes, good healthcare coverage and careful planning. With her husband at home in order to save the expense of an assisted living facility, she sought work that would help her make ends meet while caring for her husband. "It is a dilemma familiar to so many women," she said at the time—"finding work that can pay for care but also leave time for providing it." She said she had come "full circle, back to where so many women's lives begin and end—and where my career as an activist began: jobless, unsure how to pay the next month's bills, caring for a family that depends on me for survival—and utterly and deeply determined that something about our country must fundamentally change." The experience only reconfirmed her commitment to justice for all, and more recent events reinforced her belief that she, and others, must continue to speak out.

"There really is a war on women, a very nasty war," Michelman said in reference to the focus on abortion during the 2012 presidential campaign. "And the progress that opponents of women's rights have made is astounding. I don't know why there isn't a revolution in the making. The one thing I hope we can accomplish while the spotlight shines on these issues is to broaden the discussion to include the threat to women's economic security as well as to their health and rights. I will be doing some public appearances and will certainly make that connection. This is a very dangerous time for women's futures." And for Michelman, it is a time to fight for justice.

My cousin Lynn Hardy Yeakel was not marked at an early age to be a fighter for justice, equality and women's rights, although it comes as no particular surprise she turned out that way. Yeakel grew up partly in an extended family of aunts and others on a Virginia farm, and partly in the far more rarefied air of Washington D.C. with her immediate family: mother, brother and father, my favorite uncle, Congressman Porter Hardy, Jr. The added experience of education at a small girls' secondary school and subsequently at Randolph-Macon Woman's College may have offered a feminist foundation; the feminist movement was beginning to go into full swing when she graduated in 1963. Yeakel and the movement were a good fit.

There were six women among the nine of us in my generation of the Hardy family; Lynn, the youngest by nearly a decade, was always the one who was Going Places. Among the places she *almost* went, en route to her current position at Drexel University, was back to Washington in 1992 as a senator. After winning the Democratic primary in that "Year of the Woman," she suffered a heartbreakingly narrow loss to politically savvy Senator Arlen Spector, with supporters and opponents alike crediting the loss to her own lack of political expertise. Hardly skipping a beat, she went on to serve as Mid-Atlantic Regional Director for the U.S. Department of Health and Human Services during the Clinton administration. She is now Director of Drexel University College of Medicine's Institute for Women's Health and Leadership and holds the Betty A. Cohen Chair in Women's Health. Among other endeavors, in the 1970s she helped establish Womens Way, a fundraising organization designed to support nonprofits working on and for women's issues.

"I never wanted to be the typical daughter, the sidekick wife, the *Good Housekeeping* homemaker of the year," Yeakel writes in her 2010 book *A Will and a Way*. "Beyond caring for and enjoying the family I love, I learned early that it was part of my DNA to speak up and stand up for the rights of women, who for so many centuries have lived lives as second-class citizens, often denied opportunities to discover their human potential."

One of the rights Yeakel believed critical for women was that of controlling their own bodies, making their own decisions about when and whether to have children. It was a conviction formed early and acted upon with determination. In 1970, with two young children and an assortment of volunteer projects not quite satisfying her energies, Yeakel took a course called "Community Involvement."

"That's where I learned about Clergy Consultation Service," Yeakel says. "It was a statewide organization of clergy of all faiths set up to provide help and protection for women with unwanted pregnancies. I got to sit in the office of Rev. Alan Hinand, during one counseling session, and I said, 'That's what I want to do.' I was in the first group of lay counselors to take the training, in August, 1971."

The other motivation for Yeakel's commitment to reproductive rights came through two stories she tells of early experiences. When she was a 15-year-old high school student she learned of a friend from a prominent family who had gotten pregnant, and gone to New York for a $2,000 abortion. Not many years later she learned of another story, this one of a young woman without money or resources who had to end an unplanned pregnancy in a desolate room with a bare light bulb hanging from the ceiling—and was never able to have children after that experience. "What struck me was the inequity of it all. One friend with money and connections, one with neither."

Karen Mulhauser is another whose drive for reproductive choice is as strong today as it was in the early days of Roe v. Wade. Exactly 34 years to the day after she experienced a frightening, violent rape, a reminder of Mulhauser's story reappeared, in an August, 2012 letter she wrote to the *Washington Post*. Mulhauser was responding to comments about abortion and rape that swirled around Congress and the 2012 presidential campaigns. "Congress," she wrote with palpable incredulity, "is still talking about forced rape and legitimate rape and fertilized eggs with more rights than women?" Mulhauser's story illustrates both the heights of success and the extremes of humiliation and anger that can be encountered in the struggle for reproductive rights.

Mulhauser did problem pregnancy counseling in Massachusetts and worked with Planned Parenthood of Seattle, training professionals who worked in federally funded family planning programs, in the 1960s and early 1970s. She was Executive Director of NARAL, then the National Abortion Rights Action League, when the issue of funding abortions for victims of rape was under discussion in Congress. Mulhauser fiercely believed such funding had to remain in place—because she knew too well the horror of rape. She reasoned that telling her story, a terrifying incident that had happened only months earlier, would help the men on the Congressional subcommittee understand, so she volunteered to do so. She told them the story that she also shared with NARAL members in a letter and agreed to include here.

"I had been aware of the problems experienced by rape victims, and had read analyses of the psychology of rapists and their 'needs.' I had tried to imagine how I would react if ever I were threatened by rape. I imagined that I would resist."

But abstract theories went out the window on one dark, frightening night. Her husband away on business, Mulhauser was sitting alone at the kitchen table, absorbed in her work, when she looked up to see two intruders and find a gun pointed at her head. "Resistance was the farthest thing from my mind. My first thought was for my sleeping seven-year-old child. I knew I must not scream. I pleaded with them not to make noise and wake him. For two and a half hours, while they stole everything of value from our home and raped me repeatedly, I could think only of survival—mine and my son's. What would they do if he awoke, as he often does at night? Would they tie and gag him as they had done to me and force him to watch them rape his mother? What if he screamed? All these thoughts rushed through my mind. And my husband—would he return home to find us both dead? He would have to find a way to survive us.

"Nothing could have prepared me for the torment, the terror I experienced that night."

Mulhauser was helped to recover from the experience through strong support from her husband, friends and the police—and the men were convicted and given "satisfyingly long sentences." She did not become pregnant as a result, "but if I had, and was told there were no funds to pay for an abortion, I would have found some means to abort. I would even have risked a self-induced abortion. There is no way that I would be twice victimized by such a forced pregnancy."

Mulhauser wrote at the time, and says now, that although the terror sometimes returns, her primary feeling is one of anger. "I'm glad that anger is replacing terror, because I can do something about that. I am angry at the rapists, because they invaded my home, my privacy and subjected me to one of the most violent acts that one human being can inflict on another.

"But I am angered, too, by the insensitivity that I see in our society," she told NARAL members. "I am angry when I hear lawmakers like Congressman Ed Patten (who died at 89 in 1994, after serving 17 years in Congress as a New Jersey Democrat,) who said, in a conference committee dealing with the Labor-HEW appropriations bill, that the issue is not whether or not the rape was forced but how much the woman enjoyed it."

During Mulhauser's testimony, Rep. Patten "appeared to be asleep." Representative Silvio Conte (1921-1991; then a Republican from Massachusetts) turned his swivel chair away from her so that he was facing the wall. Others on the committee carried on conversations with aides. "They were obviously made uncomfortable by my story of terror and just as obviously do not know how to deal with real human beings who are desperate as a result of unwanted pregnancies."

Two weeks after Mulhauser's testimony, which she recalls as both a horror and a relief, the committee voted in closed session to cut off all funds for abortion unless a woman would die without it. If her anger needed any fuel, that surely provided it. During her stint as Executive Director of NARAL ((1975-1981) membership grew from less than 7,000 to over 135,000, the budget grew from a few hundred thousand dollars to over $4,000,000, development of a model national grassroots organizing plan was begun, and both the NARAL Political Action Committee and the educational NARAL Foundation were started. She was asked to represent NARAL and/or to debate the abortion issue with all major print and electronic media.

Now President of the consulting firm Mulhauser and Associates, she is at the forefront of national debates ranging from gun control to nuclear war to global security. And she remains fiercely committed to reproductive rights. Asked if she objected to being identified in connection with the story above, she said she would be happy for it to be re-told, especially if it can help people understand the need for abortion for rape victims. "It has so shaped who I am." As for the sleeping son? He did not wake up until morning. Now 6'3", in his mother's eye he is "a blessing and a treasure." And Mulhauser is still speaking out.

Dorothy Fadiman's voice is heard throughout the U.S. and beyond through her Oscar-nominated, Emmy-winning films focusing on social justice and human rights issues. In 1961, when she sought to end an unintended pregnancy, it was as if she had no voice at all. Fadiman was a graduate student at Stanford University. She learned she could get an abortion in Reno, for several hundred dollars. "I had $600 in the Student Union, so I cashed that out and went to Reno. I was blindfolded, and the procedure was done with no anesthesia. After I got home I was having extensive bleeding, and wound up in the emergency room. Because I had excellent care there, I recovered. But when contraception and abortion are not available, people die.

"For 30 years I was silent. But those of us who had gone to back alleys had to speak up. That's when I made *When Abortion Was Illegal.*" The powerful documentary, featuring women telling of their illegal abortions, won an Oscar nomination and a long list of awards. And Fadiman is also still speaking out. Through her independent media production company, Concentric Media, she continues to create, offering clips, mini-documentaries and full length films free through her website.

I first met Ginger Johnson in 2012, shortly after she returned from her 60th reunion at Vassar where, she reports and I can certainly believe, she had a very good time. Johnson, a tiny, stylish, white-haired woman with lively, intelligent eyes and a pretty face that seems always about to break out smiling, had shared her story earlier with me over the phone: She was teaching school and living in Washington, D.C. in 1956, and "No question about it, single women in those days did not have babies." Suspecting she was pregnant, Johnson visited a gynecologist on L Street, who was recommended by a friend. He gave her the name of a woman she later met at a lunch counter. "It was $300. I was a teacher employed by the feds. I had $300 in my retirement fund, so I cashed it in. I met with a man who had a car; there were three or four of us, all blindfolded. We drove for about an hour; I think we had to have wound up in Pennsylvania. I was fully awake during the procedure, and remember hearing a man swear about something that had gone wrong." Apparently not wrong enough to do permanent damage, though, because the women were soon driven back to the original spot in downtown Washington. "We were all so nervous, we didn't talk at all," Johnson recalls. But what she recalls best, from those days when women had virtually no voice and certainly no respect, is the remark of the gynecologist after determining she was pregnant: "For somebody with a masters degree from Harvard," he said, "you're not very smart."

Johnson is, for the record, very smart indeed. She is also an activist. She can often be found going door to door to promote political candidates and good causes. She is probably still available—since she's now retired from a career in publishing—to advise or protect women 50 or 60 years younger who seek to visit the Planned Parenthood clinics she strongly supports, and will take on the sharpest minds around in debating social justice issues. What became of the gynecologist on L Street is unknown.

Janet Denlinger, then chairman of the NARAL board, had the gavel when news came that the respected physician George L. Tiller had been killed by an anti-abortion fanatic while handing out bulletins at his church in Wichita, Kansas. Everyone in the organization knew of Tiller's work; many had known him personally, and the news was an overwhelming sadness. Denlinger had not thought of sharing her own story until that moment, "but then it just poured out:

"It was 1966, and I was starting my second summer in Boston as an intern, working as a laboratory assistant. I was just about to be 21 years old and had been accepted at a prestigious university to begin graduate studies in the fall. I was also very much 'in love' with someone who, it turned out, was not so much in love with me. In those days underage females had to have permission to obtain a prescription for the pill—and that would mean explaining to one's parents why such a prescription would be justified. That was the end of April. By June, I suspected that my luck had run out, along with the boyfriend, and I worked up the nerve to ask a friend for a recommendation for a gynecologist. The walk up Joy Street on Beacon Hill and the longer walk back to my boarding house were among the most joyless of my life. I guess I thought that the doctor would identify my 'problem' and offer some assistance—silly of me, as all forms of assistance I could use by then were illegal.

"By now I was having morning sickness with great regularity. I spoke to my former boyfriend to see if he would help, financially as well as logistically. There was a network of friends who had friends who had friends...and through what seemed like an endless process they finally found an abortionist...."

Denlinger's problems began to mount. First was the money—$400 was the price for the abortionist they finally found and it was no small sum at the time—and second were the logistics. The abortionist was in Kansas City, the only appointment that seemed available was two days later, and the only way to get from Boston to Kansas City was by train because the airlines were on strike. Critical time, with August having now arrived, was passing. A roommate eventually proved the key to Denlinger's change of fortune. "She had some money, and I had some money, and the boy finally came up with something to contribute—and my roommate and I boarded a train to Kansas City."

The next morning Denlinger and her guardian angel friend took a taxi to the Kansas City Colds Clinic, "where a masked and gowned man I hoped was a doctor met us. I gave him the money, and he gave me a pill—probably a tranquilizer—and began. I remember he told me that it would hurt more than any pain I had ever felt, which was true, and that I had lied about how far along I was, probably true. They were desperate measures for desperate times. I felt cold, hurt and scared, and as soon as the abortion was over we were literally shoved out of the door." Denlinger remembers little of some significant details like getting to the airport, because the strike had happily ended. Her friend had by now taken charge and gotten them headed back home. But small irrelevancies stay with her, woven into the grim memories of the Kansas City Colds Clinic. "I remember the dress I wore, a navy and green checked shirtwaist dress, and the matching grosgrain ribbon holding back a less-than-perfect-by-now flip hairdo."

The choice she made, Denlinger says, "allowed me to go on with the life I had invested in so far. None of my friends, other than my roommate, were aware of what went on during those two days away from 'normal' life. Perhaps the worst thing was that at that time abortion was a secret word, a dirty word, and anyone who had one would be labeled as 'loose.' My best friend had been so labeled by the small town where we grew up when she came home eight months pregnant and then married the first available man who would act as the father. I thought I would kill myself before I let that happen.

"I vowed then that not only would I initiate the conversations, I would stand by the side of anyone who needed an abortion, whatever the consequences to myself. And so I have. As a biology teacher in the town 10 miles from the one in which I grew up I was able to help girls in need of a safe place to go for the two years I taught there. It was in 1972-73, and Roe v. Wade was just happening. When I retired from the science and business world, I had the privilege of becoming a board member of NARAL Pro-Choice America. Our mission is to empower people, influence politics and develop policies to protect every woman's right to choose a safe, legal abortion and access other reproductive health care options."

More than 40 years later, in Washington for a gathering to lobby against the 'War on Women,' Denlinger met a 20-something young woman accompanying her father. "I asked her, 'What do you need to hear from us?' And she said, 'Stories. Stories from people before Roe v. Wade, for women who are having abortions now.'" That, and similar encounters with women a generation younger, are the reasons why Denlinger continues to tell her story.

And as for the women—and men—of new generations speaking out? Some of them fervently believe that life begins at conception and abortion is murder and should be banned. Those who feel that women's bodies belong to women themselves tend to focus more on reproductive rights than on the issue of when life begins. They are writing blogs about protecting those rights, mounting internet campaigns or joining activist groups.

Some are fighting hard against anti-choice campaigns that target specific groups, such as the 'Black and Beautiful' billboards linked to an anti-abortion website that went up in the spring of 2011 in largely African American neighborhoods around the U.S.:

"The issue isn't really where abortion opponents place their billboards," wrote Belle Taylor-McGhee in a *San Francisco Chronicle* opinion piece in June, 2011, "it's what they hope to gain. First and foremost, abortion opponents want to make abortion illegal—and are hoping these billboards will persuade more African Americans to support their goal. Secondly, they purport to claim some moral authority over black women's private medical decision making about childbearing.

"As an African American woman, I find the billboard campaign both racist and offensive: racist because it singles out a group of people—black women. And offensive because it dares to insinuate that black women are not intelligent enough to decide what is best for them and their families." Taylor-McGhee is national communications chair for Trust Black Women, an organization dedicated to protecting the rights of "women whose voices are not heard" on issues also including contraception and sex education.

Other reproductive rights organizations—from Planned Parenthood to NARAL Pro-Choice to Trust Women to Physicians for Reproductive Choice and Health and Medical Students for Choice—are seeing an increase in young members. As one teenager told me, after sharing the story of her struggle to access a safe abortion in midwestern America in 2009, "I've just signed up online to join NARAL Pro-Choice. It looks like the battle, for people like me, is just beginning."

# Chapter Eight

# Lifelines:
# Networks Yesterday and Today

Today, because it is a constitutional right, finding help to end an unintended pregnancy should be fairly simple. It was not always thus. And in many parts of the U.S. it already is no longer thus, if you happen to be among the millions of women without significant funds or resources.

"I think it's not fair," one young mother told me in 2012. "I have too many children already and the law says I don't have to have another. But I can't afford a doctor and I can't get to a clinic." She is two generations younger than this writer. "I don't think I'm any better off than you were in 1956. Tell me what *you* did."

What we usually did, of course, and many think we'll be doing again, was turn to other women.

In Chicago, beginning in the late 1960s, many of these women were *Janes*. 'Jane' was officially—as official as any of the women's liberation movements of the time could be—'The Abortion Counseling Service,' but if you were looking for help in the Chicago area you simply looked for Jane.

"Heather Booth started her (social justice) work in the sixties when she was in college," explains Judith Arcana, who still proudly identifies herself as a Jane. "There was no Chicago Women's Liberation Union, and no 'Jane' organization when Booth began her activism. In the fall of 1970 the abortion service that had come to be known as

Jane became a 'work group' of the CWLU—so there's some question of which came first." Booth, one of the founders of both CWLU and Jane, went on to lead *Citizen Action* and *USAction*. Record keeping was not a priority of many 1960s activists, but the history of the movement has been carefully documented in films such as Kate Kirtz' and Nell Lundy's *Jane: An Abortion Service* (1996) and books including *The Story of Jane: The Legendary Underground Feminist Abortion Service* (University of Chicago Press, 1997) by Laura Kaplan, herself a former Jane. What everyone knew and many still remember was a flourishing underground network whose members arranged, and eventually provided themselves, something over 11,000 abortions in the four years before Roe v. Wade. The Janes initially directed women to a man they believed was a doctor. By the time they learned this was not so, they had also learned that the procedure was fairly simple. The abortionist they had worked with—apparently quite skillful even if not professionally trained—helped them learn to perform abortions, and the operation shifted from his offices to several apartments of Jane members where trained volunteers performed the abortions. Illegal and risky, the underground network and its procedures were remarkably effective and safe.

Arcana, now a distinguished multiple-degree-holding teacher of literature, writing and women's studies, a performer, poet, essayist and author, might appear to have come a long way from the underground network of illegal abortion, but she is proud of her history as a Jane. And if the distance from those days is long, she has never veered off the path. Her book-in-progress at the time of this book's writing is titled *Hello. This is Jane*. Her history with the clandestine service dates to the beginning of the service itself.

"In the early seventies," Arcana says, "I thought I was pregnant and at the time that would have been bad. I discovered ultimately that I was not. But I had contacted the women of the service and one of them had called. She was very intelligent, very courteous. She said, 'By the way, we're going to be taking in new people in the fall; if you're interested, you could come. I was extremely interested, she was extremely welcoming. The meeting was held in a little church, with maybe a dozen women there. And that was the beginning of my work as a Jane."

As they grew in number and resources, the Janes would hand out brochures that began with the statement, "We are women whose ultimate goal is the liberation of women in society. One important way we are working toward that goal is by helping any woman who wants an abortion to get one as safely and cheaply as possible under existing conditions." Those conditions included the fact that abortion was illegal in Illinois, but the Janes explained that no one had been prosecuted for having an abortion, only for performing one. Their first major job had been to find someone qualified to do the procedure. There were, understandably, few doctors willing to take the risk of losing their license, but the Janes themselves were fearless. And over the course of 11,000+ abortions, reports of problems were remarkably few.

Marian was one of those 11,000+ women. "I was a freshman at the University of Chicago in 1972," she says. "My boyfriend and I were using birth control and being very careful, but I somehow managed to get pregnant. We considered getting married, but we were so young and so unready to be parents, and we would have lost our financial support. I already knew about Jane. I called the number, and soon spoke with a woman who was one of the kindest people I think I'd ever met. Within a week I had been counseled about what to do and what to expect, had had the abortion in a clean, quiet apartment and gotten my life back. My boyfriend and I married about four years later, raised two healthy children and will soon celebrate our 50th anniversary. Have I ever talked with my children—or anyone else—about that experience? No. There wasn't really any reason ever to do so. But I support Planned Parenthood and *only* pro-choice politicians, and if my granddaughters lose the right to choose you may see me out on the streets marching for their rights. Did I mention we are lifelong devout Catholics?"

Marian recalls getting the Jane brochure but not much about what it said. In fact, it was a fairly comprehensive informational piece that is much like the materials and the one-on-one counseling received by women coming to some of today's clinics that are described further on in this chapter. The brochure (and counselors, once connections were made) outlined what would happen, what kind of anesthetic might be used and how long the procedure would take. It also covered the aftercare involved including a follow-up visit to a gynecologist. "You may have some emotional 'blues' after your abortion," the brochure read. "Partly this is because of the way we're brought up; partly it's because of hormonal changes in your body. If you want to talk this over with someone, call us." The Janes may have been not only efficient and determined, but also notably compassionate.

Pat Maginnis' underground network in the San Francisco Bay area started earlier, and was, if anything, more in-your-face than Jane. Maginnis is now retired but still ferocious as she approaches her mid-80s. Asked if she ever had worries, or regrets, she snaps back, "Of course not. I'd do it again."

In 1966, after having worked hard for about five years advocating for abortion rights, Maginnis took the matter of those rights into her own hand and began passing out leaflets on the streets of San Francisco listing names of physicians in Mexico and Japan who would provide abortions. "The List," as Leslie Reagan reported in a 2000 *Feminist Studies* paper, "took on a life of its own." As word spread and demand soared, Maginnis and her colleagues scrambled to make sure that they were sending women to safe places. Though they were operating outside the law, they took pains from the beginning to guide women toward good care. Initially organized as the Society for Humane Abortion, the loose-knit group soon evolved into the more radical Association to Repeal Abortion Laws (ARAL.) Reagan terms ARAL "a forerunner of the women's health movement, which by 1974 consisted of over one thousand women's health services. As an early and outspoken advocate for women's right to abortion, Maginnis helped shape the feminist perspective on abortion law and practice."

Maginnis speaks of her childhood—she was born in 1928, one of seven children in a poor, abusive Catholic family in Oklahoma's Dust Bowl—as an appropriate formative background for the feisty activist she would become. "I went to a convent school, and that helped me see how terrible (Maginnis is free with stronger adjectives) the Catholic Church is, especially in its oppression of women. Then I had a few jobs, and then went off and joined the Army which infuriated my parents. I had a black boyfriend, and that didn't sit well with the Army so I got sent off to Panama. I worked as a ward assistant in the military hospital there. I saw one woman tied to her bed to prevent her from trying to self-abort, and that pretty much settled who I was going to become. I later had an abortion in Mexico, and while I was studying at San Jose State I wound up at San Francisco General after a self-induced abortion, with policemen standing all around asking me questions and making threats." These early adventures, which Maginnis rattles off as if she were reading from a logbook list, came together with the leaflet campaign beginning in 1959, when she was 26 years old. Within the next five years, Maginnis would team up with Rowena Gurner, "a nice Jewish girl from New York," and Lana Clarke Phelan, a southerner who was married to a police officer. Gurner had earlier had to fly to Puerto Rico for a weekend abortion and rush back to get to her job, unable to afford any more time off. At 31, she rode a bicycle from New York to California. Phelan grew up desperately poor in Florida, married at 13 and had a baby at 14. Almost immediately pregnant again she had then scraped and saved for a crude $50 abortion. Gurner, Phelan and Maginnis gained some renown, and a well-deserved place in feminist history, as The Army of Three.

The efforts of the Army of Three would have wide-ranging impact on women's health, political advances, social justice and reproductive rights, but for thousands of women it was simply a personal story. As Betty Barker explains early in the telling of her story in Chapter Four, when you needed an abortion in those pre-Roe days in Northern California, "you just knew to ask for Patricia Maginnis."

In most major metropolitan areas in the turbulent days before Roe v. Wade it was possible to get an abortion by pleading before a hospital committee for one's health or sanity. If one were required to navigate these murky waters, as is described by a number of women in pre-Roe stories elsewhere in this book, the experience was almost always demeaning and humiliating. Many physicians tried to help women follow this path, which was at least safe and legal, and not all of them had admiration for radicals like Maginnis. It's unlikely that she cared.

Loretta Ross is among those who are carrying on, today, the work that activists like the Janes and the Army of Three were getting off the ground nearly a half-century ago. Although the Supreme Court affirmed a woman's right to choose an abortion in its 1973 ruling, that has not translated into reality across the country, especially for women of limited means and resources. Many of those women are African American, and Loretta Ross is their champion.

Ross, who is co-founder and National Coordinator of SisterSong Women of Color Reproductive Health Collective, grew up in an African American family that was poor in financial resources but rich in qualities of mutual love and support. Her parents' support was key to the beginning of what she calls "my seven-year reproductive rights career." In reality, that career is still going strong.

Pregnant at 14 through incest, Ross went into the Salvation Army Home in San Antonio. "Whenever I hear those bells," she says a half-century later, "I give money. This was in the sixties, when there was no other choice but to go out of the country. My parents were poor." The home provided prenatal care; the idea was that the baby would be given up for adoption at birth. In Ross' case, though, things took a different turn. "The nurse brought my son in. I think it was a mistake; you were not supposed to see the baby. But they brought the baby in to nurse. I kept looking at him, thinking *'He's got my face!'*—and so I became a single mother. I had turned 15 by then." Ross still gets teary recalling that time. Noting that raising a child conceived through incest "is not a good way to become a parent," she nevertheless has absolutely no regrets. Her own "were great parents (despite the obvious issues with protection and birth control for their daughter) and they co-parented with me." Her son, now an engineer and a grandparent himself, is a source of pride to his mother. "He has pretty much taken over the role of patriarch."

Two years after her son's birth, Ross was off to college—and pregnant again. "My mother would not sign for birth control for me. But this time I was pregnant by my boyfriend, who was in law school and eager to pay for an abortion. Fortunately, I was in D.C., where abortion was legalized in 1970. Not so fortunately, it was late term, close to third trimester, and I had to have a saline abortion. I went to Washington Hospital Center, where I got my sister to forge my mother's signature on the permission form. I aborted twins. Meaning: I would have been a mother of three at 17. I'm always a little skeptical of these abortion regrets stories." After that abortion, Ross determined to get birth control. She obtained a Dalkon Shield IUD (intrauterine device)—and shortly afterward became one of those launching, and winning, a suit against manufacturer A.H. Robbins for the damages sustained by thousands of women who used the device.

"My first job," Ross says, "was with a rape crisis center (she was one of the first African American women to direct such a center,) where I learned that it was not my fault. Twenty-five percent of black girls are victims of some sort of abuse. Those experiences and that first job are what I call my seven-year reproductive rights career."

SisterSong, a network of 80 women-of-color and allied organizations working on reproductive justice issues, was founded in 1997 and "serves as a national organizing center for feminists of color," Ross says. Its members and volunteers also work, often around the clock, to help women of color needing an abortion. "In Atlanta we go up to 24 weeks, through the wonderful Feminist Women's Health Center," Ross says, whereas many states limit abortions to 20 or 22 weeks. SisterSong hosts women from out of town in homes and escorts them to the center. "We take a lot of what we call 'hard cases.' They are always poor, often far along in the pregnancy and they don't have private insurance." Their stories are Ross' motivation.

"Not too long ago I put up a mother of five, in her late thirties, who had spent all the money she had on a Greyhound bus ticket from Ohio, because she was too far along for an abortion there. At first, everything was fabulous. She was calm, and very sure of her decision. Her mother was looking after the children back home. She had the abortion—and then a 10-day ice storm hit Atlanta. Nothing was moving. Her mom, who had planned on getting back to work the next day, was in Ohio with the five kids going crazy. I finally cashed in frequent flyer miles and flew her back home."

Another incident was sadder and more complex, and closer to the basic issues that keep Ross working for reproductive rights for women of color. "I got a call from Chicago, where Black Women for Reproductive Justice has a fund for women who have run into a time limit. A pregnant 14-year-old was coming with her mother, who had two or three other kids at home. The 14-year-old was still sucking her thumb, her teeth sticking way out from years of this, clearly a distressed child. Turned out, they were accompanied by a man, and I am satisfied he was the child's abuser. We had one trauma after another. The child ran away, and we had to go looking for her. The mother was also obviously dysfunctional—among other things, she left her purse on the plane, with the child's birth certificate which we had to have in it. We offered birth control for the child, and the mother said—if you can believe this—'She won't need it.' There were too many echoes of my own childhood.

"People don't realize how difficult it is—the layers of regulations, lack of access, time limits—how difficult it makes our choices, how vulnerable it makes our children."

At the end of 2012, Ross planned to step down from leadership of SisterSong and return to Emory University to complete a doctorate in Women's Studies. A graduate of Agnes Scott College with an honorary Doctorate of Civil Law degree from Arcadia University, she is as passionate about the overall field of women's issues as she is about reproductive justice. "What they're teaching is very esoteric theory. I want to make it real. The fact is that there is a lack of valuing women. How can I say it—it's not just a lack of humanity in so much treatment of women, it is *de-humanizing.*"

The Feminist Women's Health Center that Ross mentions, the place to which SisterSong often shepherds women needing abortions, is about a 20 minute drive from the site of the dreary, long since demolished house where my back alley abortionist was in business in the 1950s; there are light years of good news between the two. Atlanta's FWHC started with small groups of women sharing information and learning about their own bodies. "Our founding mothers were inspired by a powerful idea," the clinic's mission/history statement reads: "to reclaim knowledge about their own body by learning from each other and ourselves through self-help. Self-help is the ability to understand, care for, and make one's own decision about healthcare. Self-help was a cornerstone concept of the women's health movement." The clinic now offers a variety of services that range from annual wellness exams to birth control options to information about fertility issues like donor sperm. And it protects the rights of women like those who turn to Loretta Ross for help in ending an unintended pregnancy. Those rights however, and the places that protect them, are fragile reeds in a turbulent storm of opposition today. Clinics such as those operated by FWHC and Planned Parenthood face competition from an assortment of 'crisis pregnancy centers,' or 'pregnancy resource centers,' where women may get pregnancy tests and counseling but no information about abortion—other than what often amounts to pressure against it. Such centers, which are often located near abortion clinics and as a rule do not include medical assistance, out-number abortion facilities by a ratio of more than four to one. Some, perhaps many, of these resource/counseling centers offer valuable services to pregnant women wanting to deliver healthy babies. Some attract women who are seeking a safe abortion, might be already in distress, and are jolted by the harsh response their mention of abortion evokes.

One such center was found by Shelly Smith a few years ago, and described to me during a dinner party at which we happened to be seated next to each other. She had been a 19-year-old student at Ohio University some years earlier, and suspected she was pregnant. Since abortion rights had been guaranteed years before she was born, the issue of an unwanted pregnancy was, to her, a non-issue: she would have an abortion, the earlier the better. Neither she nor her boyfriend (whom she would later marry) were in any way ready to have a child.

Her first task was to confirm the pregnancy. Smith looked in the phone book—this being shortly before iPhones and apps came on the scene—and found a nearby clinic that advertised free pregnancy testing, with no appointment required. Within hours, she was at the front door. "It was a welcoming place," Smith says. "Clean, nicely decorated, with comfortable chairs in the reception area and smiling women offering to help. I said I just wanted to get a pregnancy test, and was told it would take only a very short time. I was shown to a small 'consultation' room with an adjacent bathroom. I gave them a specimen and settled in to wait a few minutes for the results."

Instead of promised test results, here is what Smith got for the next hour or so:

- A video of an abortion procedure
- An 'informative talk' about fetal pain
- Additional scripted talks about the evils of abortion

"I kept asking when I could have the results of my test. They would say the results would be ready in just a few minutes; and then start another lecture or video."

Smith did get the results, which were positive for pregnancy. Her counselors would not, however, offer any information about where she might obtain an abortion. "They just asked if I understood I would be killing a baby." Shaken but undeterred, she went back to the phone book and found a clinic where she was able to end her pregnancy.

Smith says today that she believes those who oppose abortion are well within their rights to maintain 'pregnancy crisis centers.' "I just think they should say up front exactly what they are, and what they will not even talk about with you."

Two other young women who shared stories elsewhere in this book reported similar experiences that had occurred in different cities, one in the south and one in the midwest. In both cases the women had thought they were going to a clinic where they could get information on abortion. One had already confirmed her pregnancy, the other was seeking pregnancy testing and abortion information. In both cases the women eventually did have abortions—one in her second trimester—but in both cases they felt misled by the advertising that brought them to the clinic.

Another Feminist Women's Health Center, this one in Yakima, Washington, has been a beacon of help to many west coast women. It has also been at the center of a long and painful battle fought by a soft-spoken woman named Beverly Whipple. From my experience of Whipple's calm demeanor she seems an unlikely person to be in the midst of violence and danger. But over an adventurous lifetime that came to place her at the center of senseless violence she has also been an enthusiast for motorcycle riding, spear fishing, skiing and a long list of similar interests. And her heart has simultaneously been in the work of offering safe, legal and accessible abortions ever since 1979. That was the year that she and a friend, Deborah Lazaldi, opened the Feminist Women's Health Center in Yakima. What is remarkable about the gentle-mannered Whipple is the equanimity with which she looks back on the years since then. Those years witnessed provision of safe abortions, birth control services, testing and treatment of sexually transmitted diseases, and Pap smears to some 11,000 visitors a year at the original clinic and two others in Renton and Tacoma—under the umbrella of Cedar River Clinics—but they also saw repeated acts of violence: protesters chaining themselves to the building with bicycle locks, plus arson, death threats and fire bombings.

"One time, somebody kicked out a window, dumped in five gallons of gas and lit a match. Though the building didn't burn down, there was water and debris everywhere. But when women are bound and determined to have an abortion they will do so. The day after the fire, women were coming in, walking over the rubble, saying, 'I have an *appointment!*' They didn't care what the building looked like."

That determination, and the continuing needs she saw, kept Whipple going. "One woman drove to our clinic from some distance, using every dollar she had to get there. Because it was a late term abortion it was a two-day procedure. She just planned to sleep in her car. She had no money for gas to get home. So we had a fundraiser and set up a fund that we still have, to provide things like taxis, hotel rooms, food, child care, all those needs."

About the vehemence of opposition she and her colleagues have faced, Whipple says, "I'm an optimist. I have to be. I like to think that people will some day *get it* that women just need control of their own bodies. I'm still excited when somebody does get it." And she is undaunted by those who do not. "One day in the early 1990s I spoke with an Operation Rescue leader. I said, 'Don't you trust women to make their own decisions?' And he said, 'No. I don't trust women.'"

Today's professionals and volunteers working to make abortion accessible include the physicians who work often in extraordinarily difficult conditions. One fairly typical example is in the story of a 42-year-old physician I'll call Eric, who works long hours at a women's health clinic in one of the states with multiple restrictions on abortion and a very active anti-abortion population.

"I grew up poor," Eric said, when asked about why he does what he does. "I watched my mother struggle to feed too many children with very little money. She was always tired, and to me, the oldest of seven, she seemed always pregnant. I love my younger brothers and sisters, but we might have loved each other more in separate bedrooms. Or at least we might have gotten along a little better. I know what it feels like to be hungry, and to have little or no control over your life. That is the basis of my empathy for so many of my patients. I see what I do as, in a very small way, helping give them back their lives."

Eric was smart and always motivated. He seldom got in trouble as a child—"I just didn't have time"—and made top grades from elementary through high school. Scholarships and spare-time jobs got him through a state university and medical school.

"My first specialty was in family medicine," he says. "But I had always been drawn to OB/GYN and after a year in general practice I went back to complete training in this field. I would not trade it for the world."

Eric is married to a physician in an entirely different field, and is the father of a two-year-old son. His wife regularly worries about the hostility of protesters at his clinic, speaks of the violence that has injured or killed others like him, and "worries some more. It's, like, 'Do we really have to go on this way?' and then, like, 'Of course.' She is very supportive."

If his childhood experience motivated Eric to go into medicine, what motivates him to keep at it, in light of the emotional toll and physical risk? "There's an easy answer to that," he says. "The long answer is that it's never absolute, I do have qualms and fears, and occasionally I just want to quit and become an ophthalmologist in private practice. But the short answer is: my patients.

"I look at the protesters, or read the vitriol that seems to come continually from the anti-abortion community, and I want to say, 'If you could see what I see.' I see girls barely out of childhood who are not only not ready to be a parent but whose bodies are not ready to go through months of what could be a very hard pregnancy. I see women whose families are complete, often much larger already than they can afford, who know that one more baby—or another six or seven months of a pregnant mom—will tear apart the fragile fabric of the family they have. I see young women about to start a career or go to college, or who are struggling to support their parents and grandparents and would be ruined by having to continue an unwanted pregnancy. I even saw one young woman in the U.S. military who had spent every dime she and a number of family members could scrape up to get her home from active duty overseas because she could not get an abortion at the facility where she was. She had been raped by a fellow soldier, something she told me was 'fairly common and impossible to prove.' She had managed to get leave, even though she couldn't get help. She is the main support for an extended family that includes her six-year-old daughter, and she told me if she had to give up her career in the military she'd never be able to provide that support. I think it is morally wrong that we make women like the first few I spoke of go through so much to exercise their legal right to choose; I think it is criminal that any woman serving our country should have to go through what that last one did, not even having her military insurance cover the care she needs. I asked her to send me a card or note some time after she got back, but she never did. I think I can understand her not wanting any reminders of a terrible time."

"Some of my best friends and favorite family members are pro-life," Eric says. "And absolutely anti-abortion. I like to point out that I am pro-life myself, and wish that abortion could become very, very rare. But I am pro-women and pro-choice. Until such time as family planning is offered across the U.S., until contraception is taught and made available to every woman and man in the country and pregnancies resulting from rape, incest and nonconsensual sex are eradicated, I will continue to fight for reproductive rights for all women."

Today's abortion rights lifelines often come through Planned Parenthood facilities, but the organization has become such a target for anti-abortion forces that most of those involved with stories in this book are not named. Reproductive rights leaders repeatedly point out that abortion is only a tiny percentage of the services offered by Planned Parenthood and that women—and men, who can get tests and information on sexually transmitted disease amid other services—are being deprived of vitally needed care when Planned Parenthood clinics are forced to close. It does not seem to matter. Abortion has become a polarizing issue for those who see the zygote/embryo/fetus as a person and want all abortion banned. Planned Parenthood has, unfortunately, become the lightning rod for their battle flag.

Will other lifelines evolve, if the anti-abortion forces continue to make safe procedures difficult to access? "Without a doubt," says Judith Arcana. "I think there not only will be but already are plenty of places where (underground help) can be found. Women and girls must find resources, and will continue to seek out help. Sadly, they'll also have to spend an obscene amount of money. I don't know who it will be or how it will work out. There are so many dangers, especially with the increased popularity of herbal remedies. More and more women are interested in alternative medicine; I do meet them. They say, 'who will train me?'"

Arcana knows, at least, that underground networks can be developed. But the prospect of American women being pushed backward toward reproductive choices that can be expensive, dangerous and often fatal, strike her and many others as almost bizarre. "We have the best medical care in the world available in this country," says one beleaguered Ob-Gyn, "and the anti-abortion people want to see women sent back to the dark ages?"

# Chapter Nine

# Physicians Who Risked Everything— And Some Who Still Do

In towns and cities across the U.S. throughout much of the 20th century communities proudly managed to "take care of our own" in matters medical and personal. The ethos still holds in some places— if anecdotal evidence can be believed—although urbanization has undoubtedly brought changes. But today, unwanted pregnancies tend to happen disproportionately to young women who have no private physician or money to spare. Those women who are able to reach a free clinic often find a physician who is overworked, underpaid, severely tested by the tactics of those who object to his or her professional choice—and still able to offer compassionate care.

Fred Jones (a pseudonym) was a cardiologist in a southern university teaching hospital, father of three daughters born between 1948 and 1954. "For that time, especially before the '60s reached into the Southland, we were raised in a pretty permissive household," the oldest daughter said in a long, rambling conversation we had shortly after her 60th birthday. "Dad always told us that if we, or any of our friends 'got in trouble' we must come to him and he would take care of it. But we were pretty good girls and I don't know anyone he actually did help."

I went from that conversation to a visit with Dr. Jones. He is a tall, still good-looking man in his late eighties, proud of his long career—

the university recently named an endowed chair in his honor—and of his family and friends. He confirmed that the story his daughters tell is correct. "It was commonplace," he told me. "If some girl came in—often it was another doctor's wife, daughter or friend but it could be an almost-stranger—we would guide them to an Ob/Gyn we knew could be trusted and he would arrange for an 'emergency appendectomy.' I think that was probably true of most hospitals and clinics before Roe v. Wade. An extraordinary number of emergency appendectomies were performed, and to my knowledge very few physicians got in trouble about it. There were not that many decades, after all, between the time family doctors took care of their patients however they saw fit, and when Roe made abortion legal. But there were plenty of desperate women during those decades, and I hope it doesn't happen again."

What about young girls in his city who would not have known his private-school-educated daughters? Might they have come to his hospital anyway? "Not to ask for an abortion, not before it was legal," he says. "The ones I saw in the hospital were the ones who had tried to self-abort and wound up bleeding or septic, often dying. Knowing what that worst case scenario looked like was the main thing that made me want to be sure my daughters didn't risk winding up the same way." Asked what options those girls with fewer resources had, Jones says there were "underground networks" dispensing information and advice. And there was one case, he says, of an untrained abortionist being arrested after a botched abortion landed his client in the hospital, but because the woman recovered and no others came forward, "I think the case was dropped. We (physicians) did know there were people like that."

Dr. Jones considers himself, then and now, "pro-choice, but just not an activist. There have been too many other battles to fight," he says, "and frankly I've had my hands full juggling some of them while trying to make a living."

At about the same time that Fred Jones was advising his daughters to avoid any risky behavior if they 'got in trouble,' a young third-year medical student named Kenneth Edelin was called to the emergency room of Nashville, TN's Hubbard Hospital at three in the morning, where he watched in helplessness as a young woman died. "It still sticks with me," Edelin says today, "though that was a very long time ago." His experience was not something one would easily forget. As described in his 2008 book *Broken Justice: A True Story of Race, Sex and Revenge in a Boston Courtroom*, the death of the young woman Edelin guessed to be about 17 at most was sudden, gory and unpreventable by the time she reached the emergency room. She had been left at the door by someone who did not stay, and she was by then consumed with infection caused by a botched abortion. The strip of tubing left when her uterine wall was pierced—probably by something like a knitting needle—was still inside her. Edelin writes of the sounds, smell and feeling of overwhelming sadness he felt while watching the attending resident hold his patient's hand as she died.

His own mother's death from cancer at the age of 46, when Edelin was 12, had propelled him toward a career in medicine focusing on women's health; the scene in the Nashville emergency room would help steer him towards obstetrics and gynecology. And that latter choice would almost land him in prison for many years.

Now retired and living in Florida, Edelin was Chief Resident in the Ob-Gyn clinic at Boston Community Hospital in September, 1973, shortly after passage of Roe v. Wade, when a young woman he calls Evonne was admitted. She was well into the second trimester of her pregnancy. A frightened, 17-year-old high school senior, Evonne was accompanied by her mother and asking to have an abortion. Her mother's fear of what Evonne's father would do if he found out about the pregnancy reinforced the apparent urgency. Doing the abortion was an easy decision, "well within hospital guidelines, my personal guidelines and the law," Edelin recalls. But it turned out not to be a simple procedure. When a saline injection indicated trouble, Edelin performed a hysterotomy. At its completion he removed a tiny fetus that had been dead for at least several hours. That was on October 3, 1973. The following April, he was indicted for manslaughter. An all-white jury would find the young black physician guilty by the time the sensational trial was over a long and agonizing year later. And by the time that decision was reversed, Edelin and his supporters would undergo a long and complex struggle.

Edelin's ordeal was about more than abortion, as is made clear in his own exhaustively detailed account in *Broken Justice*, as well as in news accounts of the time. The initial investigation was tied in with Boston's anti-busing movement, Edelin's anti-abortion foes were joined in the battle by the Catholic Church, and more than a few details suggest there were old fashioned personal issues like jealousy and vindictiveness swirling around from the beginning. The trial was high drama about a tiny fetus and a lot of big, scientific words, with excruciating attention to details like where, exactly, the clock on the wall was positioned. But at its heart was the issue, still in question today, of who should decide what is best for a patient other than the patient and her physician. It was also the first time after abortion became legal that the enormous potential danger to physicians and reproductive rights activists alike was made evident. Later fully cleared, Edelin came dangerously close to losing his license and his future for performing a necessary medical procedure.

Pamela Lowry, whose own brush with the law a few years earlier is described in Chapter Two, was among the abortion rights activists pitching in to support Ken Edelin. Then the coordinator of the Pregnancy Counseling Service in Boston, she and others immediately began drumming up support and raising funds to cover the costs of an adequate defense. It would be led—and eventually won on appeal—by famed civil rights lawyer William Homans, who suffered a heart attack after it was all over. (Homans recovered, and continued to fight for civil rights for many more years; he died at 75 in 1997.) Possibly because the eventual outcome was a happy one—Edelin went on to a distinguished career as physician and teacher—there are lighter moments in the memories of some who were on the scene. In files Pam Lowry dug out to help with this book, is a hand-written letter from Bill Homans in which he rewrites a scene from Hamlet to recount the trial. It concludes: "...then we will be stung by his tears and stricken to our souls by his voice. Failing that, we must appeal. (Trumpets, offstage.)"

Since the day that the Supreme Court's decision in Roe v. Wade made it legal for women with unwanted pregnancies to choose an abortion, opposition has never ceased. The intensity of the opposition can be distressing, and often frightening, to women seeking to exercise their rights; for physicians and others trying to help them it can be deadly.

Dr. David Gunn (1946-1993) of Pensacola, Florida became a target of Operation Rescue in 1992, his name, phone number and image appearing on 'Wanted' style posters plastered on walls and windows around town. Operation Rescue, a large, well financed national Christian organization whose website proclaims its mission is "to restore legal personhood to the pre-born and stop abortion in obedience to biblical mandates" denied circulating the posters. An anti-abortion rally was held at Dr. Gunn's clinic one morning in March, 1993, organized by John Burt, a lay preacher at Whitfield Assembly of God Church. During the rally a protester named Michael F. Griffin stepped from the crowd and shot Dr. Gunn fatally in the back. Burt told the press that protesters had no intention of harming Dr. Gunn. Michael Griffin was convicted of the crime and sentenced to life in prison.

Not quite one year later, in July, 1994, Dr. John Britton and a clinic escort, James Barrett, were shot to death outside of another abortion facility in Pensacola. Barrett, a retired Air Force lieutenant colonel, had just picked up Dr. Britton from the airport. Widely known anti-abortion activist Paul Hill, who described himself as a retired minister, fired a shotgun at point-blank range into the front seat of the pickup truck where the two men sat. Barrett's wife, in the back seat, was wounded. Hill, who termed the killings "justifiable homicide," was executed for the crime on September 3, 2003.

On December 30, 1994 two other innocent people died at the hands of anti-abortion crusader John Salvi. Shannon Lowney and Lee Ann Nichols were receptionists at clinics in Brookline, Massachusetts. Salvi confessed. He committed suicide at the beginning of his sentence.

Four years later, off-duty police officer Robert Sanderson was killed when the abortion clinic in Birmingham, Alabama where he was working as a guard was bombed. Eric Robert Rudolph was convicted of that crime—along with the bombing of Centennial Olympic Park in Atlanta. Rudolph received two life sentences.

Dr. Barnett Slepian worked 15 to 24 hours a week at the only abortion clinic in Buffalo, NY, performing abortions on mostly poor clients. The 52-year-old physician was shot to death on October 23, 1998 in his Amherst, NY home with a high-powered rifle, by anti-abortionist James Kopp. Kopp, caught three years later in France, apologized to Dr. Slepian's widow.

Dr. George Tiller, whose Wichita, KS clinic was targeted by abortion opponents for many years, was shot to death while handing out bulletins for the morning service in the foyer of his church on May 31, 2009. The following January, Scott Roeder was convicted of first-degree murder for Dr. Tiller's killing.

Those stark realities form a constant background to the daily lives of abortion providers today, many of whom endure taunts, threats and harassment on a daily basis.

Willie J. Parker, MD, MPH, MSc is a Washington D.C. based obstetrician who travels monthly to Jackson, Mississippi to perform abortions at the only clinic in that state. Dr. Parker speaks of the intersection of work and spiritual convictions in the following chapter; his travels to Mississippi dovetail with a belief in social justice. "I do this out of respect for the law, and respect for women," many of whom need the option of abortion, he says. But it is a risky business. There are always angry protesters positioned around the clinic, blocking the corner and access gate and trying to prevent women from entering; and the protesters often direct much of their anger toward abortion providers. So why would he keep at it, when he's got plenty of work to do at home?

"Physicians in Mississippi cannot afford to work at the clinic," Parker says; "it's just too great a risk. I fly to Jackson, get a car and drive to the clinic. There is a security guard inside the gate, so I've never felt physically threatened." An incident not long ago, however, altered his sense of security.

"During a down time one morning I walked across the street to a sandwich shop," Parker says. "The merchants are supportive of the clinic and the people in the community are friendly and neutral. They resent the protesters and wish they'd just go away. After I sat down I realized one of the protesters had recognized me and followed me across the street. She positioned herself about three feet from me and was trying to get a picture. I put my hands up so she couldn't photograph my face, and she eventually left. When the people in the shop asked what was going on I explained that I was working at the clinic. They said they wished they had known; that they'd have made her leave.

"As I was walking back across the street after finishing my sandwich the woman appeared again, came quite close to me and began to say things like 'How much are they paying you to murder babies?' Then, because I'm African American, she started talking about how I was committing genocide against my own race."

Parker, an open-hearted man with a reputation for compassion (as well as for speaking out,) was beginning to have a hard time ignoring his pursuer. "I tried to resume my posture of indifference, but she was quite close, and now she was making racist remarks—that are also absolutely false. The 'black genocide' is part of the campaign of intentional misinformation; they're quite comfortable with half-truths, which are easier than blatant lies. This was the first time someone had been in my space, though, interfering with my ability to move freely. I realized I am going to have to be more careful."

Dr. Nancy Stanwood, an Ob-Gyn who also offers her thoughts on faith and reproductive rights in the following chapter, says she has never felt threatened because providing abortions is part of her women's health practice. But she laments the stigma that still surrounds abortion. "You just so often hear people say 'I don't know anyone who has had an abortion,' because women don't talk about it. That's like 20 years ago when you'd hear people say they didn't have any gay friends—because their friends were not out yet. I do believe there is a great danger in the stigma, in keeping quiet."

Stanwood believes the physicians who don't face danger owe a special debt to those who do. "I think we have to support each other," she says, "in every way possible, and I think we have to keep building support among others. Doctors have got to be there for women struggling with the very complex issue of abortion." Stanwood cited a story she had recently recounted to Lola McClure, a registered nurse and blogger for hairpin.com: "I had a patient who had an unplanned pregnancy, and she thought she and her partner could make it work. She was getting prenatal care, but at 20 weeks she found out that he was married, had children with his wife, and also had children with another woman. She had to totally re-evaluate her life plans. She had two children from a previous relationship who were a bit older, and she had been in a partnership to raise them, and now she was looking at, 'Do I have this baby while I'm with this big fat liar? Do I have this baby alone?' ...I am, again, day by day, impressed by the genuine concern and thoughtful deliberation of patients referring to this issue, and I was so impressed by her careful thought process and that of her family and support people. She did decide to have an abortion." The story, Stanwood says, illustrates how complex the decision can be, and how important is the provision of abortion as part of the continuum of care. For this professional care to be unavailable in areas where doctors must take huge risks to provide it is, she believes, morally wrong.

Another physician who saw his role as abortion provider—primarily to poor and disadvantaged women—as both a moral and an ethical necessity was Arkansas Ob-Gyn Willliam F. Harrison, who opened the Fayetteville Women's Clinic with a colleague in 1972. For this author it was a great disappointment not to be able to talk with Harrison, who died in September, 2010, soon after I began work on the project. His was the first name mentioned by countless leaders of the reproductive rights movement, whose automatic response to news of this coming book was, "Talk to William Harrison!" From all reports, he was undaunted by threats and vilification. His clinic was firebombed, vandalized, blockaded and routinely picketed. But as reported in his obituary in *The New York Times* Harrison's commitment to making abortion available, particularly to disadvantaged women, was total. It had begun with a woman, "black, poor and middle-aged—(who) had come in 1967 to the Arkansas hospital where Harrison was a medical student in obstetrics. A doctor, after examining her swollen belly, had told her she was pregnant." The woman's reply, "Oh, God, doctor, I was hoping it was cancer," made an indelible mark on the young physician. His obituary cited his decision, after delivering more than 6,000 babies, to devote himself to providing abortions, "writing that if he wanted them to be legal, safe and available, the only moral and ethical course was for him to do them. As for the protesters frequently outside his clinic, he often said they were splendid advertising, drawing women in need to the clinic who might otherwise have not known where to go."

There were other, earlier physicians who willingly took risks to provide abortions because they saw the need and believed they should fill it. Probably none was more interesting, or in many ways less likely thanks to his openness, than Robert D. Spencer of Ashland, PA. Dr. Spencer opened his small-town practice in the 1920s, treating miners, housewives, families and children for every known disease—(and Schuylkill County had an abundance of them all.) He went down in the mines when accidents happened. He distrusted religiosity, and governmental interference in people's lives. And by his own admission the good doctor had performed more than 100,000 illegal abortions by the time of his death in 1969. He was moved by the stories of women (and occasionally their male partners) who sought his help, stories that were later collected and made into a documentary, "Dear Dr. Spencer." Those stories, also reported in Vincent Genovese's biography of Spencer, *The Angel of Ashland: Practicing Compassion and Tempting Fate,* range from quaint to poignant to desperate, but Spencer routinely responded. It was a time long before protest lines around community clinics, but not without peril. Spencer was arrested three times. He died before the last trial was completed but was never convicted of wrongdoing, quite possibly because he had helped so many people from one end of Schuylkil County to the other that no one could be found who would vote to convict him of anything.

Dr. Nathan Rappaport was not so lucky in his trials. Rappaport was also unlucky in having a practice easier to target, and in being outspoken about it all. After graduating from the University of Arkansas Medical School and completing advance training at the University of Pennsylvania, Rappaport opened and operated a lawful practice in Jackson Heights, NY in 1926. It was only a few years later, though, that he veered off the legal path. As he explained to Village Voice writer Marlene Nadle in a 1966 interview, "I always believed that competent abortions were essential, but when I first opened my office in 1926 I never thought I could go outside the law to commit them. I sent all my abortion patients to another doctor. Two years after I was in practice a relative begged me to perform one and I finally did it on the kitchen table. Then the Depression came. More and more women asked me for abortions because they could not afford to feed another mouth. The collections from my practice had dwindled to almost nothing. There was pressure from my family to take the abortion money. By 1933 I had let the druggist and other doctors know I was available and made abortion my specialty."

By the time of Nadle's interview Rappaport had spent nine of the previous 15 years in jail, had lost his license, his home, his family and his reputation. He had performed abortions over a period of 40 years for rich and poor, black and white, victims of rape and mothers of too many children. He did not feel it was his job to pass judgment on the woman's decision not to bear a child. Rappaport told Nadle he was working on a book under the title of "Man's Inhumanity to Woman," but there is no record of its having been published.

Today's abortion providers, many of them women, currently have the law on their side. Legality, though, carries no guarantees against harassment or danger. Protesters often encircle clinics or gather with signs and shouts that can be frightening to patients and doctors alike; for many providers their job becomes a physical and emotional challenge. That was the case for Emily Godfrey. About the worst moments she has endured she says, "I just try not to think of them today," but it is clear the terror, and the hurt, are still with her, just below the surface.

Godfrey, an Ob-Gyn in her early forties, had planned to be a doctor from the time she was a child. Heading toward a career in family medicine, she graduated from the Medical College of Wisconsin and began a residency at Chicago hospital where victims of gang violence and of the afflictions common to poor neighborhoods frequently wound up. Among these, when Godfrey was on her obstetrics rotation, were cases that filled her with sadness and frustration. Sadness because she saw so many unwanted children or children of drug-addicted mothers brought into the world, and frustration because she couldn't do anything to help. "I did know that an IUD could be safely inserted right after delivery and that many women would have welcomed such a good way to keep from getting pregnant again. But Medicaid would not pay for both procedures done the same day. It made no sense."

Godfrey went from Chicago to the University of Rochester on a Family Planning Fellowship. She was still intending to pursue a career in family medicine. But during her fellowship years, while working with the World Health Organization in Nicaragua and Mexico, she became aware of tragedies such as those cited by other physicians throughout this book: women all over the globe who are suffering and dying from botched abortions. "That certainly reinforced my convictions about the need for both contraception and safe abortion. To keep things like this from happening." After returning to Chicago and while looking for a position on a medical school faculty, Godfrey took a one-day-a-week job at an abortion clinic in Rockford, IL, about 90 miles north. It was the only place within miles where a woman might get a safe abortion. Soon, protesters were circling the clinic, shouting epithets and threatening harm to both prospective patients and clinic doctors. She was frightened, but kept working. It was 2007. Finally, one midwinter day Godfrey had a patient who needed to go to the hospital. The Ob-Gyn on call was not available and Godfrey was rebuffed with an insult when she tried to negotiate with the hospital on her patient's behalf. She called her friend Dr. George Tiller for advice, and he told her how to get her patient the help she needed by sending her to the hospital in an ambulance. Both the patient and Godfrey survived. But for the young doctor, already frightened by the angry protesters, being treated with hostility by hospital staff was humiliating. Not long afterward, having taken a job as assistant professor of family medicine at the University of Illinois, Godfrey stopped working at the Rochester clinic. Two years later, Tiller was killed.

Most of this was detailed in a cover story that ran in the *New York Times Sunday Magazine* in 2010, which featured Emily Godfrey on the cover, to her considerable dismay. Young, brown-eyed and pretty, with a stethoscope around her neck she makes a great cover girl for an issue featuring a major article on 'The New Abortion Providers.' But she is quick to explain, "I did not agree to be on the cover. I did give them that quote about being a Catholic girl from the suburbs and liking calm and serenity. The story was about abortion providers; I am a primary care doctor who does abortions." Other than the unwanted focus, Godfrey does not regret speaking out for reproductive rights. "I know how essential it is that women have the right to a safe abortion. It is a global human rights issue," she says. "I am very, very concerned." But about the hostility and dangers she faced? "I knew and loved George Tiller," she says. "It all got to be too much." Soon after the *Times* article appeared, Godfrey accepted a teaching job in another state where she maintains a busy schedule with less visibility.

Three other women physicians, all currently active as abortion providers in states where restrictions are many and protesters constant, offered stories and comments for this chapter. Each is affiliated either with a hospital or a clinic. They have faced varying degrees of difficulty in following the profession they have chosen, and been extensively trained to do. One said she would not mind being identified, but in light of the heated emotional atmosphere I am calling them Doctors A, B and C.

"I am very lucky because my husband is also a physician," says Dr. A, "and not only does he understand but his job lets me stay home a good bit of the time. But it is very, very difficult to have to contend with the vitriol of the protesters when I go to the clinic. I go directly from there to my patients, and there is just such a disconnect. These women are often overburdened with too many children already and cannot handle the thought of adding one more. Some of them are simply too young to be bearing a child, let alone trying to raise him or her. One young teenager said to me, 'They called me a murderer. This baby's daddy really is a murderer. He's going back to jail soon. I am so scared to have to go back through those people.' It broke my heart. She didn't seem scared of the man who got her pregnant—whoever in the world he is—or even scared of all the other cards stacked against her by our society, but she was scared of the people who wanted to tell her how to live her life." Dr. A told her patient to wait until closing time. She gave her a ride to the bus in her car so the girl would not have to face her antagonists again.

For Dr. B the issue is not so much physical or emotional struggle as it is pure hassle. She is probably going to stop working as a provider. "Where I trained and where I now practice the laws are similar: they require the physician to give the patient 'a right to change her mind' within 24 hours. What this means is that I would have to spend two hours every day calling women, answering questions, delivering required messages. For example, the law says you must tell the woman that if she has the baby the father would be responsible for child support, even if he's paying for the abortion. Did this ever change a woman's mind? No, never. What makes me angry is we're treating women like simple, non-sentient beings. More restrictions don't seem to be lessening the occurrence of unwanted pregnancies, just making it more and more difficult for women with unwanted pregnancies to get safe, professional help in terminating them." Dr. B did not take this thought further, but there is only one direction it can go: if obstacles to safe abortion become insurmountable, women will follow unsafe paths.

Dr. C said her problem "is from within. I have a really bad temper." It finally got the better of her, after several months of intermittent encounters with hostile protesters who gathered at her clinic. "Sometimes they would be at the front entrance, then they would disappear for a while, then they would reappear around the parking lot. Everyone at the clinic agreed simply to keep our heads down and pay them no attention. But one day—this was several years ago—I had just had it. As I got out of my car there was a grim-faced woman with a 'Baby Killer' sign quite nearby, and she shouted something at me that pushed me over the edge. I walked right up in her face and started lecturing her about my rights, and my patients rights, and about how many unwanted children there are in our town who could use a little care and attention if she had nothing else to do but stand around holding up a sign and interfering with lawful medical practice. I was very calm and sedate at first—I think that caught her off guard so she didn't immediately respond. But I started talking faster and faster, and I could feel my face getting red and my blood pressure rising, and all of a sudden I realized I could get into some serious trouble. So I spun around and walked as fast as I could to the clinic door. She was still shouting as I slammed it behind me. My first patient that day was the most beautiful, gentle-mannered young Hispanic woman. She had three very young children and her husband had left her, knowing she was pregnant with a fourth. She said she didn't think she'd be able to count on him for support. Before she left she came up to me and thanked me. She said, 'You saved my life.' Well, after that the protesters didn't seem to matter."

A constant return to focusing on their patients is the common thread in conversations with physicians who are working as abortion providers today. Some of them like Doctor C and Willie Parker do face potential personal danger, some are not personally threatened but work to support their colleagues "on the front lines," as one phrased it, in every way possible. Almost all express concern—but their concern is for their patients.

David Eisenberg, MD, MPH, is an example. Eisenberg is on the faculty of Washington University School of Medicine in St. Louis, where his work encompasses family planning and contraceptive counseling, obstetrics and gynecology and an assortment of related fields. In a conversation about the state of reproductive rights today, and projections for the future, his comments veered toward despair, and his stories tell why:

"There was one 15-year-old, a ward of the state, pregnant after non-consensual sex with an older boy. Because her case had been assigned to Catholic Charities the ACLU had intervened by way of judicial bypass. On the day of her abortion the case worker basically abducted her in order for her to have the legal abortion which Catholic Charities opposed. The emotional and mental distress for a 15-year-old who had already been a victim of assault was unimaginable.

"In Missouri, teens must have parental consent, which can get people in trouble. Often that means telling things that they don't necessarily want to tell. I also know teens who have been accused of murder for having an abortion.

"The voice that's been missing from the debate is that of women. If we could only change the perception, focus on women. People like my mom, who had an abortion in 1971 when she already had a five-year-old and a two-year-old. She had to go to a psychiatrist who would say she needed it.

"Or take the 30-year-old woman who came to me at our hospital, with something severely wrong with the fetus at nearly thirty weeks, asking, 'If this baby survives, is there a chance of any meaningful life?'

"Women face these difficult issues. Women should be supported, not judged. Instead, we just have more and more laws."

Those stories are not unlike the stories told by Robert Spencer at his trials more than a half-century ago, or the stories Willie Parker thinks of as he shields his face from camera-wielding protesters in Jackson, Mississippi in 2012. The voices behind their stories are the voices of women they see.

I asked Dr. C if she were thinking of going to work somewhere else.

"Every day," she said. "I think about it every day. But if I give in, and quit, they (the protesters) win. I don't really lose, because I can go to another town, another state, and get a good job. But women lose."

# Chapter Ten

# What's God Got To Do With It?

"I prayed and prayed," she told me. Her voice sounded like that of someone younger than her 17 years. "First I prayed that I wasn't pregnant. Then I prayed for, like, something to happen, anything. Then I just prayed for help. I wanted to pray for forgiveness, but I couldn't do that, because I had already done wrong and now I was about to commit a major sin."

This was Priscilla's report to me. Her older sister Mary, who now volunteers with a church-related abortion support service, first offered the story and then, with Priscilla's permission, gave me the teenager's cell phone number. Priscilla and Mary are the daughters of deeply religious parents, brought up in a church that believes life begins at conception and abortion is murder. When she went off to college, Mary began to question what she describes as "the rigidity of my parents' beliefs, and their refusal to accept even the smallest deviation from what they saw as Biblical truths. I had begun to see one 'truth' on one page of the Bible and another on another page. My parents would point to their page and call me a sinner and an apostate. So my attempts to have a dialog with them would invariably end up with their making these accusations, shouting down my own arguments and going off to their room to pray. Usually, I'm afraid, over my fallen soul." The family arguments continued and tensions built throughout Mary's sophomore year. In the summer following that year she left home, moved to New York, found a job and essentially ended most ties to her parents. "We would exchange Christmas gifts, and occasional notes or phone calls over some small issue, but we became more like casual acquaintances than family. The initial hostility just sort of faded into a polite distance. I married, finished college, kept working; I would let them know about things, but except for one trip home when my uncle died I just moved on and never looked back. My husband and I joined a spiritual community that is open and welcoming to all."

When Mary left home, her sister Priscilla was still in elementary school. "I'd always been fond of her," Mary says, "but there was too much distance between us to say we were ever close. The day she called to say she was pregnant, and didn't feel she 'could really look after a baby,' I had not spoken to her in at least six months. I just sat there and listened. She cried and cried, and spent a lot of time in between talking about 'how awful' she was. She was just a child. Finally she got around to saying she wanted 'to not have the baby.' She could not bring herself to say the word 'abortion.' But I finally did, and said I would help her if that's what she decided to do." Eventually, Mary offered to give Priscilla a trip to New York for her coming birthday. During the visit Mary forged her name as legal guardian on the required documents and saw Priscilla through an abortion.

"It was the God thing that made me so mad the whole time," Mary says. "She kept coming up with 'but God says...' while she was beating herself to death with teenage guilt and angst. And I would say, 'Whose God? Isn't my God just as good as yours? My God would never condemn somebody like you for choosing not to wreck her life, and not to bring an unwanted child into a world of trouble.' But Priscilla never bought that."

Slightly more than a year later Priscilla told me that she does not regret what she did but has terrible guilt about "committing such a sin." Her best friend knows and "has forgiven" her; she has told no one else. She rarely communicates with Mary, though she says she's grateful that Mary tried to help her. She cannot imagine ever telling her parents. Her pastor? "Not in a million years."

When I talked with Mary and Priscilla I was only dimly aware of Exhale Pro Voice, and had not yet heard about Connect and Breathe. Either might have been able to help her by offering a sympathetic listening ear, but Priscilla, for now at least, is primarily listening to her parents and her church leaders. Whether or not they would listen to her without judgment—if she chose to try to tell them her story—is hard to know. Exhale is a San Francisco-based organization founded in 2000 by and for women who have had abortions and dedicated to "the emotional health and wellbeing of women and men after abortion." Among its programs is an after-abortion talkline which was expanded in 2005 into a daily, national, multilingual service. New York-based Connect and Breathe is closely patterned after its West Coast nonprofit sister organization.

I learned about Connect and Breathe, which was started by the Reproductive Rights Task Force of the First Unitarian Universalist Church of Rochester, NY, in a conversation with church member Nancy Stanwood, MD, MPH. "I didn't really have anything to do with it," Stanwood says, "other than to sit on the sidelines and cheer them on." But her involvement in, and gratitude for, First UU of Rochester is boundless. Stanwood's faith journey from "unchurched childhood" to deep commitment to Unitarian Universalist principles, is somewhat like big sister Mary's journey, though Mary started out as what might be termed "fully churched." As young adults, both began to question, and to seek religious community. Both became involved in reproductive rights. Each sees herself as a deeply spiritual human being.

Nancy Stanwood's grandmother, whom she describes as "a feminist and progressive thinker," was raised in the Catholic Church but left it as a young adult and became involved in Unitarian Universalism. She raised her three children as Unitarian Universalists. But Stanwood's mother, after marrying an Episcopalian, never found a church in which the two parents wanted to raise their own children. Dr. Stanwood grew up without any formal religious home but with a general understanding of Unitarian Universalism. She wrote of her initial visit to First UU of Rochester, in an article for The Religious Coalition for Reproductive Choice, "I knew I'd found my home. The first time sitting listening to the sermon—not yet knowing anyone—I cried with relief and hope. The sense of connection and common purpose in pursuing social justice was overwhelming." Believing that a woman's right to choose fits within the broader area of social justice, and that abortion is an issue relating to women's health, Stanwood has performed abortions for her patients, when they so choose, ever since the beginning of her medical practice. As to her own choice of obstetrics and gynecology, Stanwood says, "some people go to medical school know-ing exactly what they'll do. I was not one of them. But I was drawn to Ob-Gyn because of the wonderful mix: acute care, intermediary and long-term care. As far as performing abortions goes, I see it as part of my professional duty. Our patients bring their whole lives into the exam room, and some (with unintended pregnancies) do come from faith traditions that stigmatize abortion." Often, after carefully listen-ing to her patients ("That's a hallmark of care," she says) she gives them a brochure about 'Connect and Breathe' to take home. "They need to have a non-judgmental listener."

Unitarian Universalism, characterized by some as humanism or a lifestyle with spiritual dimensions, is often cited as the far-left, pro-gressive end of the spectrum of mainline faith traditions in the U.S. At the other end of the spectrum, as it arcs over abortion rights, are congregations such as the Southern Baptist church in which Priscilla, the young woman in this chapter's opening story, is still active. Main-line Protestant churches in the U.S.—including Methodists, Episco-palians, Presbyterians and others—have some congregations that lean toward liberal views on the issue and others that take a more conserva-tive stand. Fundamentalist Protestant congregations, Roman Catho-lic and Mormon churches staunchly oppose abortion. The 'Christian Right,' currently a major U.S. political force, includes a broad array of congregations and faith-related groups solidly opposed to abortion in-cluding Focus on the Family, founded by psychologist James Dodson; the American Center for Law and Justice, Evangelist Pat Robertson's Christian Coalition; and international groups such as the Mormon-led Family Watch International and the Roman Catholic Human Life International. Their stories are rooted in long-held doctrines and their arguments—as well as their often graphic protest materials—focus on fetuses. Somewhere in between discussion of the fetus—when it be-comes a person, when it may feel pain, when it might survive outside the womb—and the stories of the woman in all the complexities of her life, is a common story that might be told. But it has yet to be heard. "I teach my students," says Nancy Stanwood, "that we need to get out of the cultural debate. It is all black and white. Our patients are living in shades of gray. The shouting is 'Baby-killer!'/'Woman-hater!' but we must focus on keeping women healthy."

In an interesting contemporary development, ultra-conservative forces on the Christian right have allied themselves with atheist Ayn Rand, thanks to the enthusiasm for Rand's writings—and for her political and economic theories. But Rand would have had a lot to say about these admirers' anti-abortion views and none of it would have pleased them. She would also probably have said it very loudly, timidity never having been one of her attributes. In *The Voice of Reason*, Rand proclaims that "an embryo *has no rights*. Rights do not pertain to a *potential*, only to an *actual* being. A child cannot acquire any rights until it is born." And abortion, she maintained, "is a moral right, which should be left to the sole discretion of the woman involved; morally, nothing other than her wish in the matter is to be considered. Who can conceivably have the right to dictate to her what disposition she is to make of the functions of her own body?" Beyond her affirmation of women's rights, of course, Rand would have maintained that God has nothing to do with it either, since she believed no such spiritual being or power exists.

Anti-abortionist Scott Roeder, who shot Dr. George Tiller as he was greeting fellow parishioners in his Lutheran church in Wichita, Kansas in 2009, did not profess to be acting on behalf of any religion or religious belief. And no religious group other than a few on the farthest-out fringes of society supports the murder of an adult to prevent what they see as the 'murder' of a fetus. God's name, though, is often invoked by those who shout about "Baby-killers!"—less often by those who shout about "Woman-haters!"—and religious fervor can be frightening in this mix. Scott Roeder, now serving a life sentence, drove away from Tiller's church in a blue car with a Jesus fish on the back.

"Dr. Tiller's murder really affected me," Sister Donna Quinn told *Religion Dispatches* writer Sarah Posner in March, 2012, nearly three years afterward. Posner interviewed both an abortion provider, who is Catholic, and Quinn, whom Posner describes as "a nun, feminist activist and former clinic escort (or as Quinn describes herself, 'peacekeeper') at a clinic on the south side of Chicago." Sister Quinn's escort service eventually brought a rebuke by her order. Catholic parishioners, who had been encouraged to protest outside abortion clinics including the one where the Sister was active, reported her to the local Cardinal, ending that particular segment of her activism. But by no means all: Quinn continues to work hard for the National Coalition of American Nuns, the Women-Church Convergence and the Religious Coalition for Reproductive Choice—Illinois, and to advocate for equality for women within the Catholic Church. "I want to call the church as I have been for years to leave its totalitarian way of governing its people," she told Posner. The church should "respect the right to dissent. Do not excommunicate, silence or expel those who work for justice, particularly reproductive justice."

One woman who wishes she had known Sister Quinn was a mother of four who sought an abortion at a Texas clinic recently, having to pass through a group of hostile protesters to do so. "I consider myself a good Catholic," she told me, "and I sure would have welcomed a nun to walk with me. Instead I went alone, and it was both frightening and demeaning. Good for Sister Donna." As to her fellow Catholics in Chicago who reported Quinn to the Cardinal, this mild-mannered young Texas matron said, "That's their right. The church tells them they are doing God's work. I just do not feel God said I had to carry that troubled, unwanted pregnancy to term. Ask any of the vast majority of Catholic women who use contraception and/or have abortions. We do not consider ourselves bad Catholics; we just do not believe in blind obedience to erroneous, non-Biblical teachings."

If most Catholics practice birth control, as is widely reported, and many identify themselves as pro-choice, abortion remains a sin in the eyes of their church today. In an effort to understand how the church deals with the issue on a personal level, I talked at length with a close friend who was born, raised and educated in the Catholic Church, entered the priesthood after seminary and now pastors a major urban congregation. "Yes," he said, "it is a mortal sin and is followed by excommunication. But if a woman comes to me I listen very carefully, trying to be sensitive to her soul. If she is considering abortion, I will, again, listen to her, but I will counsel her on other options. If she is asking forgiveness, I will help her find ways back into the community; nothing like this is ever final. What's important is to remember that no one is ever outside the circle of God's love." This good priest's openness and compassion are much of why he remains special to this lifelong Protestant. We do not, however, talk politics. He also directed me to Project Rachel, a national Catholic organization "offering hope, healing and forgiveness after abortion." Project Rachel reaches out to those who have chosen abortion, but does not condone the choice.

A Catholic woman physician who also spoke with Sarah Posner for her March, 2012 article on 'The Role of Faith in the Lives of Abortion Providers,' also questions whether there is Biblical basis for the Church's current anti-abortion stance. The doctor, who grew up a practicing Catholic and currently has a medical practice in the South, told Posner that "the Catholic Church has changed its position on abortion multiple times," and that she herself feels "its current stance is arbitrary, a kind of man-made construct," adding that she "didn't find anything in the Bible to make me think it was black and white."

Dr. Willie Parker also came from a childhood religion that taught abortion is wrong. A gregarious, energetic and widely respected African American Ob-Gyn, Parker says he struggled with the issue as an adult. "But it was the stories of the women who came to me who eventually changed that," he says. "I came to believe that abortion was an integral part of those women's lives, and other women's lives. I'm not just religious, I am a strong believer in social justice; eventually I felt it was morally wrong *not* to provide abortions within my medical practice." Parker grew up in Birmingham, AL, leaving at 18 for Berea College in Kentucky, going on to get an MD from the University of Iowa, a Masters from the Harvard School of Public Health and a Masters of Science in Health Services Research from the University of Michigan where he also completed a Fellowship in Family Planning. Until he began to struggle with the issue of abortion, there was little in his education and training that would have been in conflict with the church in which he was raised. "It was a traditional Protestant Baptist Church, with a very fundamentalist stance," he explains. "There was nothing explicit in my upbringing, just the implication that abortion was wrong." The words of another African American Southern Baptist helped change Parker's mind.

"It was a sermon by Dr. Martin Luther King," he says. "King said that what made the good Samaritan 'good' was that instead of thinking about what might happen to him if he stopped to help the traveler, he thought about what would happen to the traveler if he didn't stop to help. That led me to a deeper understanding of my spirituality, placing a higher value on compassion. I couldn't stop to weigh the life of a previable or a lethally flawed fetus against the life of the woman sitting across from me."

Some of the stories that still reinforce Parker's conviction that abortion is morally right involve women who were only children when he saw them. One had been molested by an uncle who was staying with the family, but because she was "a child with a very quiet demeanor, which her parents saw as good behavior, she had concealed the pregnancy until she was 19 weeks along. It was terminated at 20 weeks." Another patient was an 11-year-old who was brought in by her grandmother. The grandmother had found out about the pregnancy a few days before the beginning of the child's sixth grade year. "It was not incest, not coercive, just premature sexual activity." Asked if he knew what became of either of these patients the doctor says, "No—and that is in some ways ideal. The fact that I've not seen them again leads me to believe they have been able to have normal lives."

His conviction that abortion is also a social justice issue is closely tied to Parker's empathy for the poor and for women of color. "A disproportionate number of women who die from unsafe abortions are African American," he says. "In New York 70 percent of the women who die from unsafe abortions are African American or Puerto Rican. We have lost the narrative of the women who are dying."

Parker also performed an abortion on a 32-year-old attorney, senior staff for a prominent U.S. Senator. "It was her first pregnancy, and she and her husband were very excited about it. But we found out in the 21st week that the fetus had a lethal, severe developmental abnormality. The woman later had a subsequent pregnancy with the same lethal anomaly, diagnosed earlier, which her own Ob-Gyn took care of. The fact that she was able to conceive again, and to go on with her life, those are the important facts." Dr. Parker's work as an abortion provider, his work with family planning and public health are all, he believes, firmly within his spiritual beliefs.

Rabbi Peter Stein, whose e-mails bear the bottom-line quote from Exodus Rabbah 19:4—*(A)ll are acceptable to God. The gates are open at all times, and all who wish may enter*—has a similar strength of spiritual conviction. The women in Stein's life include a mother, a wife, a sister and ("especially") a daughter; all of whom he wants "to have the personal freedom to make decisions that are right for them. Too often, sadly, in the Orthodox community and in other places, women's freedoms are controlled by men—husbands, fathers, physicians. Banning abortion has the effect of banning women's ability to be in control of their bodies and their lives. That's not equal, and it has driven a lot of my concern."

The rabbi's other driving concern is for freedom of religion. "So often, attacks on abortion rights and access become violations of (the constitutionally ordered separation of) church and state. Since my religion permits it, I don't want a law that prohibits access because of another religion's teaching."

Stein has plenty of backing. "In Jewish law and tradition there are several layers. The first is, of course, the Bible. My stance and the Jewish point of view generally begin with the law in Exodus 21:22 ff. This is the section that establishes capitol punishment for one who takes a life but a lesser punishment—a fine—when one causes a miscarriage. The principle is that a fetus is not a full human being; legally, it has no juridical personality of its own. It is a serious matter, something to be considered very carefully, but it is not the same. In the context of medical abortion, too, it is something to be considered very seriously, not to be done for frivolous reasons, but it is permitted because it is not the same as the taking of a life."

Rabbi Stein cites Jewish teachings from the Talmud going back to the 4th and 5th centuries that say therapeutic abortion is permitted "up to the moment of crowning" if the mother's life is in danger. "The principle," he says, "is that we sacrifice a potential life in order to save a full life—whereas we don't save one life for the sake of another. There's also another Talmud passage that says the fetus is 'as the thigh of its mother'...not a separate life until it is born." Other stories reinforce his belief that the mother's life is paramount. "(They) deal not with the physical well being of the mother but with her emotional well being...if she is suicidal during the pregnancy, if she is distraught over learning that the fetus has Taysachs or another disease—the answer generally in these cases is that abortion is permitted because of the mother's anguish, again because hers is a full life and the fetus is (only) a potential life."

One woman whose story is told in an earlier chapter is a devout Jew now in her late seventies. I contacted her as this chapter was underway to ask if she had any thoughts she'd like to add, and she listened carefully as I read the paragraphs above. She said she thought she would like to have Peter Stein as her rabbi, but is perfectly happy with the religious leaders she does have—"and I'm sure they would all agree with him.

"But when I had my abortion in the early 1960s? Religion had absolutely nothing to do with it—other than the fact that my parents were upstanding members of the community, and I was unmarried, and great embarrassment would've come about at temple and everywhere else. That's why I took the route I chose, dangerous as it was. I can't imagine that anybody would have considered me 'sinful,' I was just an unfortunate kid in an untenable situation. Although I wasn't that far past my bat mitzvah and most of my friends and relatives were observant Jews, whether or not abortion was theologically okay was about the farthest thing from my mind. Now that I have two grown daughters—and a new granddaughter!—all I can say is I hope they will always have the right to choose a safer path than the one I was forced to take."

Roz Jonas, whose story is told in Chapter II, recalls the humiliation she felt, "not being able to tell my own parents, or mention working for a congressman," and the relief when her menstrual periods returned and life went back to a modified normal. But an experience a few years later sealed her commitment to reproductive justice. "I married the year that Roe v. Wade became law," she says; "I waited a long time to have kids." When she did become pregnant with their first child, Jonas went to see an Ob-Gyn recommended by a friend. She was shocked and dismayed when he treated her not with sympathy and professional kindness but "was mean, abrupt and rude." Only later did she figure out that her earlier abortion, immediately evident to the new doctor, was the cause of that treatment. "It took me a while," she says, "to realize that he was a Catholic."

The Catholic position on abortion, as with the position of the rest of the 'Religious Right,' is basically rooted in the theory that life begins at conception and the fetus must therefore be protected at all costs. Those in the pro-choice camp, whatever their theological underpinnings, would be likelier to support the views of the Rev. Scotty McLennan, Unitarian Universalist minister, Dean of Religious Life at

Stanford University, author of *Finding Your Religion: When the Faith You Grew Up With Has Lost Its Meaning* and *Jesus Was a Liberal: Reclaiming Christianity for All*. McLennan is the real- life inspiration for cartoonist Gary Trudeau's 'Dude of God' character in the Doonesbury comic strip.

In an article titled "Breath is life," printed in the Unitarian Universalist's *UU World* publication in November, 2009 McLennan re-told a story he says still affirms that core belief. "I'll never forget the sight of each of my children emerging into the world blue and lifeless," he wrote, "being struck on the back by the doctor, taking their first breath, and becoming ruddy-colored as they began crying their way into life. Now they were tiny people. Now they had joined the human race, not before.

"I don't necessarily try to reconcile my beliefs to those of others," McLennan says, "as try to keep the dialog open. We all want to reduce the incidence of abortion; beyond that you have to have sex education, good prenatal and child care. Most of us who are pro-choice have the ultimate goal: for abortion to be safe, legal and rare."

Rev. McLennan traces his theological rationale for abortion from far back in the Judeo-Christian tradition, much of which has long held that "the embryo or fetus is seen as potential human life, but not as fully human until birth or until some stage in fetal development well past conception." He adds that "there is nothing explicitly said in the Bible about abortion. Zero." But the business of breath as life, which McLennan says is part of this tradition, is often cited by rabbis. The reference starts with the creation story in Genesis 2:7: "The Lord God formed man from the dust of the ground, and breathed into his nostrils the breath of life; and the man became a living being." Orthodox, Conservative and Reformed rabbis sanction abortion under widely differing parameters, he says, but leave the decision to the woman, to be considered thoughtfully and prayerfully, and "recognizing how difficult the decision often is.

"I'm personally part of that large Protestant community that believes that human life and personhood begins at birth," McLennan says. "Some of my feelings admittedly may stem from the connotations of the words 'birth' and 'conception' with which I've grown up within the church. After a strong religious experience we might say

we've been 'born again,' but not 'conceived again.' We celebrate birth-
days, including Christmas as the birth of Christ." On the other hand,
it seems religiously important to me to be very concerned about potential life, not just actual life. The nine months of pregnancy for an
expectant mother is a very important time of preparation for the baby-
to-come and, ideally, of careful monitoring of maternal and prenatal
health. Fetal life is a magnificent continuum of development from the
zygote at the time of conception to the manifestation of the embryo at
about fourteen days, to the formation of what we call the fetus at about
three months. Of course, for those first two weeks it's not at all clear
that the zygote will become a singular embryo, much less a human being. Two-thirds of the time, the zygote doesn't develop into anything
at all. Sometimes it develops into a tumor. Or it could become an embryo, or more than one if it splits into twins. Once it's an embryo, it'll
be a long time—another 22 weeks or so—before it reaches viability
or the stage of development when it might survive outside the womb."

That line of reasoning is what leads McLennan to say he personally
thinks "the Supreme Court got it right in 1973 in terms of protection of potential life. During the first trimester—when abortion could
occur with an IUD, a morning-after pill, RU-486, or minor surgical
procedures—the decision to abort is entirely the woman's. In the second trimester, with quickening, human shaping and the necessity of
more complicated surgical procedures, the state has a right to regulate
medical procedures to protect the health of the mother. By the third
trimester, though, the potential life has become viable; since the fetus
could now live outside the womb, the state has a right to protect that
potential life by prohibiting abortion except to preserve the life of the
mother."

In search of a comment about abortion and Muslim women, I asked
Iftekhar Hai, President of the United Muslims of America Interfaith
Alliance, if he could summarize the teachings of his faith. Hai quotes
Catholic author/theologian Hans Kung in saying "'Islam is such a vast
religion, it has to be studied in different time zones, namely Past,
Present and Future' Thus any generalization about abortion would be
subject to the same scrutiny—and would result in different interpre-
tations." But with that caveat, Hai says many Muslims would permit
abortion in certain cases, primarily when it is necessary to protect the

mother's life. He cites first the Qur'an on the sanctity of life: "'*Whoso-ever saves a life, it is as though he has saved life of all mankind, and whosoever kills a life, it is as though he has murdered all of mankind.*' (Qur'an 5:32.) But various schools of Muslim law accept that abortion is permitted when life of the mother is in danger," Hai notes. "This is the only reason accepted for abortion after 120 days of pregnancy. There is also a generally accepted rule that a fetus is not any form of life until God entrusts in it a soul. Some schools of thought say the soul enters a fetus after 40 days and some say after 112 days or 16 weeks."

Reproductive rights issues have roiled many mainline Protestant denominations in recent years, along with gay rights and, to a slightly lesser degree, death with dignity issues. Most liberal churches remain pro-choice (within specified limits) and the more conservative churches adamantly anti-abortion. Many fundamentalist congregations are embracing the 'personhood' theory, which holds that life begins at conception and the fertilized egg is therefore endowed with all rights and privileges of human beings. In the case of a pregnant woman, this pits the pre-born against the already born, and the pre-born wins.

"The essence of the Presbyterian Church USA stance on abortion," says Rev. Deborah L. Wright, "is rooted in our primary belief that 'God alone is Lord of the conscience.' Hence we, and I, fully support the right of a woman to make her own prayerful and ethical decision concerning an unwanted or ill-advised pregnancy." Wright, who in the 1970s became one of the first women to be called as an associate pastor to a major church within the PCUSA, referred this Presbyterian author to church documents for more on its official position. That position urges continuation of pregnancies where "viable life" can be expected, but includes the specific admonitions that there should be no limits on access to abortion, while there should be unlimited public funding of abortion. The support of public funding parallels church support of the responsibility of religions employers to offer all forms of legal healthcare coverage to women: to make the coverage available, and leave the choice to the woman. Where their more conservative brethren refer to the fetus as 'a person,' PCUSA officialdom speaks of 'viable unborn babies—those well developed enough to survive outside the womb if delivered.'

In a group discussion with four friends who identify themselves as "spiritual-not-religious"—none wanting to be further identified—there was heated commentary on the title of this chapter. The flash point essentially boiled down to this: Whose God? And does anyone really have a corner on God or what he/she believes?

Probably not.

# Chapter Eleven

# **Family Lore**

Our mothers…their mothers…their grandmothers…these are the storytellers. Many of their stories were filled with danger and intrigue, passed on from generation to generation along with tales of bravery and adventure. Stories of struggle and success, of comedians and eccentrics have always been the stuff of family lore. But except for the occasional outlandish black sheep, stories of shame and suffering have more often been left to a whispered, vanishing past.

My cousin Pat David, who lived and died in the mountain town of Lynchburg, Virginia, was the one who most often whispered the dark family secrets to me. During my family's long summer visits to Lynchburg in our childhood we would huddle on padded blankets, beneath quilts that smelled of cedar chests and safety, watching the rain on distant mountains from the upstairs porch. As darkness settled over our open-air beds, Pat would start talking in a low, spooky voice. Pat's parents were divorced, something scandalous in itself in the 1940s. Because of that, and the fact that she was a year or so older, I considered her worldly and wise beyond measure. It was not until long after we had finished raising children of our own that she answered my question about memories of her never-mentioned father. When he wanted something of her mother, she explained, he would hold Pat by the ankles and dangle her out the window of their fourth-floor apartment. Pat was not quite four when she and her mother escaped from that horrific existence and went to live with her grandmother, my great aunt Henny. To her own children and grandchildren, Aunt Henny was known as DearMama, the two words run together to create the title that fit her well, Dearmama. It was pronounced almost without the first syllable, as D'rMAma. Dearmama was unfailingly kind and generous, but gossip was her staff of life.

"Dearmama told me," Pat would begin, "that her cousin Sam didn't really get killed in the war. He got caught stealing from the General Store, and they think he might have killed somebody in another robbery, too. He was in the penitentiary in Richmond but nobody would go see him because they didn't want to be found out..." These stories could morph into ghost stories, Sam's knife-wielding form drifting about, looking for relatives who abandoned him in his hour—or decade, or longer—of need.

And then there were the stories of young girls who were *sent away.* Cousins who had names, faces, histories, that often came to an abrupt end. Dearmama didn't want us to be *sent away.* I had only the dimmest idea of what all that entailed, but Pat sometimes spoke of what happened to young girls who refused to be sent away. They would have to drink great quantities of foul-tasting liquids, or sit in the bathtub and have boiling water poured on their stomachs. Or have lye funneled inside them. Sometimes they simply "bled to death."

I remember only one personal encounter with the phrase "she bled to death," other than Pat's sinister tales of young girls who refused to be sent away. In my mother's early 20th century yearbooks from Randolph-Macon Woman's College were sepia photos of tennis teams and gym classes, the women decked out in bloomers and middy shirts which were the athletic uniform of the day. Several photos I was often drawn to featured my mother, one of her sisters, and their best friend. The friend had long, blond curls tied with a huge bow. One day, when I was about 12 or 13, I asked what had become of the friend, and was told that she died before graduation. "Oh, my," I said, "what happened?" Sudden illness that led to a quick death was common in those days, but my mother didn't say her friend had cancer, or influenza, or a devastating disease. She said, "She bled to death." I didn't push very hard for a full explanation, but it was one of those mysteries that capture the imagination of young girls and I did pursue the issue with "but *why??*" and "how *could* someone...?" Further questions, though, evoked only the same reply, "She bled to death." It stuck in my mind because the conversation was so close to the time when my menstrual periods began; when that happened I was certain I was beginning to bleed to death. Because my mother was rooted in Victorian mores—my older sisters soon rescued me from the bleeding-to-death fears—it was never possible to find out the story of the friend who bled to death. But if I could resurrect my mother's ghost today I would bet money that she could confirm the friend was the victim of a botched abortion.

Those scenarios from the distant past represent attitudes and circumstances that are almost beyond comprehension for anyone born after 1950.

"Women today," says Ramona, "don't have a clue." She is reflecting on her own experience, and on contemporary mindsets more than a quarter of a century later. "Anybody under 40? They just cannot imagine."

Ramona was 17 and a senior in a Michigan high school in 1972, the year before Roe v. Wade would begin to make life not quite so difficult for young women caught in similar circumstances. Second in a family of five, daughter of a city-employee father and churchgoing mother who were widely known and respected in the community, Ramona's primary concern that year was mastering the notes and maneuvers for an upcoming marching band performance. Until she discovered she was pregnant. Her boyfriend, whom she would later marry, was several years older; neither felt in any way ready or willing to have an unplanned baby. "Mike said, 'I'll marry you if you want,'" she recalls; but it was the last thing she wanted. "I think we went to Planned Parenthood, and to several referral services and the pastor of some church, all of whom said they would help if we wanted." That help, though, could not be found in the State of Michigan. So after getting confirmation from her mother's gynecologist that she was indeed in her first trimester of a pregnancy, Ramona and Mike arranged a flight to New York, where a legal abortion could be obtained at the time. "There was a hospital there set up so that was all they did," she recalls; "a woman could come at any stage."

The couple boarded a flight which was met at the airport by a bus that would take them straight to the hospital. The abortion would be an outpatient procedure and they would return that night. When the doctor examined her, though, he said she was in her second trimester and would need to have a dilation and curettage (D&C), a surgical procedure requiring an overnight stay—and parental consent. Distraught, and still pregnant, Ramona boarded the plane back home with her boyfriend. By the time they arrived, her parents had called Ramona's best friend, who had driven the couple to the airport. "And she wasn't going to lie to them," Ramona says with a laugh now. "So she said, 'They've gone to New York to have an abortion.' By now my parents know, and I walk in the door, and it is not a pretty picture." Mike was banished from the house. In the ensuing days an understanding Episcopal priest helped Ramona's mother come to terms with the situation with some emergency counseling, and soon mother and daughter were on another plane to New York. They returned to the same hospital where, now with parental consent, Ramona stayed overnight and had the required procedure.

Her own story played out with ups and downs and eventual happy endings: she was allowed to have a graduation party, although it was initially denied; Mike was allowed to attend. Several years later, after he enlisted in the Navy, they were married. Neither of them ever regretted the decision not to have children.

A parallel story made a lasting impression on Ramona. "I had a roommate at the hospital in New York, an African American woman who was considerably farther along than I. She told me she had three children already and could not afford any more. But she had had to wait until she saved up the money for the abortion. I remember thinking, 'Here I am, a clueless little white girl…'" Other images crowd the memories of that time: "I had done this awful thing. Even though my parents later grew close to Mike, there was just so much guilt. Eventually, we moved back to Michigan, and I had some sort of a breakdown. And then one day I said, "You know, I'm over it."

How much difference would it have made if a legal abortion had been possible in her hometown? "Huge. I would've gone sooner, it would've been simpler—and my parents would never have known." Family issues were not only with her parents. By the time the entire episode was over, Ramona's siblings were subtly drawn into the drama. One incident offers a glimpse into the varied ways abortion could affect family relationships in those complex pre-Roe days. It happened during an argument about money to be spent on graduation parties. Probably like high school seniors everywhere, Ramona thought more should have been spent on her festivities. "Yeah?" said a younger brother about their father's reticence to come up with more; "well, he paid for your abortion." They were difficult days in countless ways.

"Women will find a way," Ramona says. "But people who think women have an abortion just because it's an easy way out simply do not know what they're talking about. Even if you know it's the right decision, it is a difficult one. Criminalizing it again would just make it more difficult again." The memory of her hospital roommate's hard decision and unnecessarily dangerous time, still haunts her.

Mo Sansing, whose experience was just a few years earlier than Ramona's, looks back on those days, and her family story, with wide open eyes and a touch of wry humor. "No right answers," she says, "but no regrets.

"At the end of 1966, I got pregnant the first time I had sex. My boyfriend had been involved with another woman, so he went to the doctor and got birth control pills for me. But we were dropping acid, and in those circumstances you tend not to think about the pills in the drawer. And oh, he said he might have gonorrhea. Conceived on acid—not a fertile field for having a baby. He said, 'What are you going to do?' I said, 'Kill myself.' I think I might have killed myself. Truly. (Instead) I told a friend in chemistry lab, a French Haitian whose brother had gotten girls pregnant."

The friend recommended a place in Mexico, "Clinica Arzate, just over the border from Nogales, TX. They said it would cost $500. My friend told her father she needed $500, didn't say what for; another friend scraped up some money and I got a check in the mail. High drama. The friend from chemistry lab drove me across the border; we left at 5 in the afternoon for an 8 AM appointment. We had to smuggle money in, drugs out. The thing about the clinic is, I went to a doctor back home who said they'd done a really good job; they called later and wanted me to recommend that clinic.

"Children? I turned out to be a crazed druggie/alkie, and felt too out of control to have kids, so I never stopped birth control. Broke up with my boyfriend, who later had testicular cancer. Somehow seemed fitting."

Five years ago, Sansing—who is actually sane and sober—told the story to her mother. Her mother, who died three years later, said she was really sorry Sansing had to go through such an experience. "But honey," she said, "thanks for not telling me then. I couldn't have handled it."

Susan Wicklund, a physician committed to women's reproductive choice, recently published a poignant memoir, *This Common Secret: My Journey As an Abortion Doctor.* Co-written with Alan Kesselheim, the book details Wicklund's years working in abortion clinics in the 1980s and 1990s, having to walk through angry crowds shouting "Murderer!" and "Baby killer!," having to hire a bodyguard to walk her home and back and to field threatening letters that the police ignored until finally the threats got deadly and specific. One letter-writer did go to jail, but the angry protesters were protected. After a brief try at doing things she loved less than helping women deal with accidental and unwanted pregnancies, Dr. Wicklund is back at work.

Wicklund was motivated in part by her own experience with a legal but utterly harsh and un-caring abortion clinic; legalization of abortion did not assure across-the-board excellence of care. "We try to make very sure that everyone seen in our clinics—for any service, not just for abortions—is treated with kindness and courtesy," says one Planned Parenthood state official. "But the reality is that there is no law that can guarantee sympathetic behavior. There are all sorts of reasons today why women get less than sympathetic treatment: patient overload, job-related stress and the necessity of hiring office staff who may not be fully 'in synch' with the right to choose, to name just three." In Wicklund's case it could have been any of those reasons, or others. But the Planned Parenthood executive (who did not want to be named) believes there are many sites today where abortion is safe and legal—and harsh. Young Susan Wicklund determined to offer something better for women wanting to terminate their pregnancies.

When she had finished her medical training and begun work as an abortion provider, Wicklund was interviewed on CBS TV's "Sixty Minutes." As the day of its airing neared, she faced the moment she most dreaded: telling her favorite grandmother precisely what she was doing in her medical practice.

"Flower Grandma" was one of the most beloved members of Wicklund's close-knit extended family. She got her name from Wicklund's toddler daughter Sonja, who needed a way to keep her multiple grandmothers separate. Since there were always flowers blooming around this particular grandmother's small home, she became Flower Grandma to Sonja—and soon to everyone else.

Wicklund tells this family story in *This Common Secret*. She speaks of the growing dread she felt as she drove to Flower Grandma's home, entered the familiar living room and sat down to explain what kind of work she was doing. She was not far into that explanation, however, when Flower Grandma began stroking the back of her granddaughter's hand and telling a tale of her own:

When she was 16 years old, Flower Grandma began, her best friend got pregnant.

"I always believed it was her father that was using her," she said, "but I never knew for sure. She came to my sister, Violet and me and asked us to help her."

Wicklund listened in silence, thinking of everything she had read about women self-aborting and dying when safe, legal abortion was not available, and of the women she saw in her clinic who often had to overcome great difficulties to end an unwanted pregnancy. She thought, too, of the women who had used dangerous home remedies in attempts to self-abort, combinations of potentially lethal herbs that were believed to force a miscarriage. Many of these women had gotten to her clinic; she knew many others had died. "I felt myself tighten and withdraw," Wicklund writes, "anticipating what Flower Grandma was going to tell me."

"The three of us were so naïve," the story continues in *This Common Secret*:

> "We knew very little about these things, but we had heard that if you put something long and sharp 'up there,' in the private place, sometimes it would end the pregnancy.
>
> "We closed ourselves, the three of us, in one of the bedrooms late one morning. We didn't talk much, and she didn't ever cry out in pain. It took a few tries to make the blood come. None of us spoke. We didn't know what to expect next, or what to do when the blood kept coming. It was all over the sheets. All over us. So bright red. It was awful. It just wouldn't stop.
>
> "We put rags inside of her to try to stop the bleeding, but they soaked full. We all three stayed in her bed. We didn't know what to do.

"We stayed there together, unable to move, even after she was dead. Her father found us, all three of us, in the bed. He stood in the doorway, staring. No words for a long time. When he did speak, he told my sister and me to leave and that we were never, ever to speak of this. We were not to tell anyone, ever. Ever."

Flower Grandma had been stroking Wicklund's hand all this time, staring straight ahead. When she reached the end of the tale, Wicklund writes, "(She) stopped stroking my hand and sat still before turning to look directly at me. "That was 72 years ago. You are the first person I have ever told that story. I am still so ashamed of what happened. We were just so young and scared. We didn't know anything."

Wicklund writes of having been left with tearful feelings of sadness and anger. "I couldn't picture my grandma as someone responsible for the death of anything, much less her best friend at the age of 16. She had carried this secret all her life, kept it inside, festering with guilt and shame. I wondered if the pregnancy was indeed the result of incest. Would it have made a difference? What were friends and family told about the death? What had they actually used to start the bleeding? What had the doctor put on the death certificate as the cause of death?" Wicklund was still turning those thoughts over in her mind when Flower Grandma spoke again:

> "I know exactly what kind of work you do," she said, "and it is a good thing. People like you do it safely so that people like me don't murder their best friends. I told you how proud I am of what you do, and I meant it."

Wicklund's grandmother and my own mother were of the same generation. The possibility of data-gathering or documenting what they knew of their contemporaries' abortions is long gone. And with it, the stories of uncounted thousands of women who died from botched abortions, either self-induced or performed by untrained friends or often well-meaning strangers.

When I decided, at the age of 77, to write this book, the first problem I faced was how to tell my family. The youngest of four girls, I had learned much and feared little from my sisters. Virtually no problem ever presented itself to me—and I was problem-prone for as far back as I can remember—that one of my sisters could not solve. They also frequently bailed me out when needed.

My sister Mimi, one year ahead of me in school, was the closest person to my heart for three quarters of a century. Husbands, children, lovers and friends would come along and claim large chunks of my heart, but Mimi was there from the day I was born: companion, collaborator, protector—Sister, in every best meaning of the word. In the winter of 1956 we were sharing a small house in Atlanta with several other young women. It was a boisterous, happy time. The number of housemates varied from month to month as people changed jobs, moved away or married, but Mimi and I shared a room—and virtually every small detail of our lives—for nearly two years in that merry rental house on North Fulton Drive. She knew of my escapades on and off the job, and sometimes we talked of how I worried about some of the men who made passes at me during job-related events when I was functioning as both public relations representative and de facto hostess. Women in those days were expected to "look after themselves," and Mimi and I were raised in both a family and a society that expected girls to remain virgins until marriage. Boys, on the other hand, could do whatever they pleased. Men, regardless of marital status, who were attending away-from-home conferences could also at least try to do whatever they pleased with whomever they pleased. Much of my job with the American Petroleum Institute involved setting up these conferences.

While she and I shared virtually every prosaic or dramatic detail of our lives, Mimi died without ever knowing the story I tell in the first chapter: that I had been raped after a business cocktail party in Sea Island, Georgia and—even more shameful—had an abortion. I took the bus to town, alone, to meet the abortionist. The next day, a Sunday, I told Mimi and our other roommates that I was having terrible cramps and thought I'd stay in bed. On Monday I went to see the Ob-Gyn whose help I had vainly sought before I took that last-resort step. For more than 50 years I kept this secret from almost everyone. At the time, and for most of those years, the whole, sordid episode was so filled with shame, guilt and the horror of narrowly-escaped criminal consequences that it was impossible even to share with the person who was my sister in soul as well as kinship.

The decision to begin work on this book, precipitated by the death of my admired friend Trish Hooper, was made only a few weeks before a family reunion planned as a memorial celebration for Mimi and my oldest sister Jane, both of whom had died in the preceding 18 months. During those several days I decided to take a deep breath—a whole bunch of deep breaths, as it turned out—and share the news of the book and my own motivating history with my remaining sister Helen, my brothers-in-law, nieces, nephews, long-grown children and assorted others. Most of them took a few deep breaths of their own and cheered me on. My husband, whom I married years after being divorced from my children's father, had long known the story and enthusiastically championed the book.

But Mimi's daughter Leslie, the age of my own older daughter and someone especially dear to me, gave me pause. I know and respect her deep commitment to a particularly conservative brand of Christianity, and we share a mutual love and honor of each other that even allows for occasional discussion of religion without argument. This, however, was something else. One afternoon during the reunion I found a chance for us to have a conversation.

"Leslie," I said, "you may have to pretend you don't know me. But I've started work on a book that I hope to publish in the next year or so..." Then I told her the general plans for the book, and my own story from beginning to end. She listened carefully, and paused before offering a response.

"You know, Frannie," she said, "I do believe that life begins at conception, and that abortion amounts to killing babies. But I think I have to believe that someone in the circumstances you were in should have an option." It was a way of offering understanding without condemnation. I am satisfied that our conversation did not result in my beloved niece's renunciation of her convictions, or in any way affect what is a strong and abiding religious faith. It is simply a family story, part of the complex family lore such as every storyteller in this book can claim.

Margaret Spaulding's choices in the days she sought an abortion were hardly more than mine. But hers is a family tale unique in many ways despite the similarities that can be found in countless stories of life before Roe v. Wade.

"Leona was born on Valentine's Day, two weeks late," Margaret says. "But she shouldn't have been. In some sense she shouldn't have been, at all."

"When she was born, on a rainy night in a tiny fishing village on the central California coast, in a house converted into a cozy doctor's clinic, I was 19 years old, a recent college drop out, married for four months to her dad, who was finishing his senior year at a state college.

"We lived, if you could call it that, on less than $100 a month for the four months before she arrived. I had resorted to a form of dumpster diving, rescuing food scraps discarded by my well-intentioned but clueless mother in law. I'd want to say, please don't throw out apple peels; I need to eat them. I worked, standing up for eight hours a day, at a local drugstore, clear through my due date. Jim worked nights as a custodian at the college.

"It was 1962 when I conceived her, on a beach in summer. Abortion was not legal and for folks as poor and naïve as we, not an option. I tried to abort Leona in my third or maybe even fourth month. What did I know? Someone said you could do it with a combination of turpentine and some kind of bark…the resulting nausea and excretions did nothing, thankfully, to deform the fetus, nor, perhaps less fortunately, to destroy it.

"She was still an 'it' then. Let's be clear; she was an 'it' until she was born. And I have loved her every second of her life. But, she was very unplanned and for some months, very unwanted.

"Playing 'what if' has never been my game. I play 'what is…' But, considering what might have changed in my life if I had been able to abort her safely…well, that's a big question. I wanted to be a journalist. I probably would have considered law school more seriously. Always a quick student, smart (in school, if not so much in life) and would likely have become a lawyer.

"Eventually, 10 years after her birth and after two divorces, I did finish journalism school and began to earn a modest living. But, my focus had to be on caring for, supporting, my little girl. So, instead of concentrating on a career, I concentrated on getting by, making do the best I could. That turned out to involve a lot of turmoil and several husbands.

"What about my daughter? She somehow survived the hardships of our early years, survived being a latchkey kid, survived the invasion of mom's 'boyfriends' and the unsettling nature of serial husbands. She survived my temper, my depressions, my chronic withdrawal and my emotional abuse, as a too-young single parent who did not have a village to help, didn't even know we both needed a village.

"But we've both been through a lot of therapy and are still working on a relationship that could have been richer, in emotional as well as material ways. She defines her life as happy and who am I to say it's not. We love each other and keep working on ways to express it.

"If I had it to do over would I try again to abort her? Yes, absolutely. I did not want a baby when I was 19 and I know I would have been a better parent if I had waited. I would also have been a wiser person, more self assured, less dependent on men to provide a life for both my daughter and me. Am I glad she survived? Of course. But if we have a choice between survival and all the advantages our minds and spirits are capable of, let's opt for the bigger life, the richer life, all the advantages we can create."

Margaret's daughter Leona is smart, pretty, capable, industrious and my favorite anarchist. I don't actually know any other anarchists, but if I did I'm certain Leona would still be my favorite. Here's what she has to say:

"I'm proud of my mom for trying to abort me. It shows her independence. I'm proud of my mom." That pride goes three ways, including Margaret and me.

In 1992, when Leona was 19, she found herself pregnant for the second time. The first time, she had an abortion; she knew she did not want children. But this was before any medical alternative was legal and she had only the surgical option. She found it unpleasant and invasive—"that whole process was sucky, as you can imagine" is the precise phrase she uses today in reference to surgical abortion. In 1992, she was aware of RU486, then known as "the French abortion pill" which prevents a fertilized egg from implanting in the uterus. Leona was determined it was the alternative abortion she wanted and should have.

Without sharing any details of the plans with her mother, and with financial assistance from local activists, Leona boarded a plane for London. There she acquired a bottle of 12 pills for her personal use. She was accompanied by Dr. Louise Tyrer. A distinguished OB-GYN physician who had founded the organization now known as the Association of Reproductive Health Professionals, in 1992 Dr. Tyrer had just retired as Medical Director for Family Planning International Assistance (of Planned Parenthood Federation of America.) But she was not ready to retire from family planning activism.

When their return flight arrived at JFK Airport in New York, Leona and Dr. Tyrer were met by a small group that included author/activist Lawrence Lader, founder of the organization that became NARAL-Pro Choice, and later of Abortion Rights Mobilization. Their reception committee also included several lawyers retained by Lader—and a few U.S. Customs officials who promptly seized Leona's pills. No one was really surprised by all this. The trip was a test case of the Food and Drug Administration's prohibition against importing the drug that had, at that point, been successfully used by more than 110,000 women in Britain and France

Across the continent in California, it came as a surprise to her mother and step-father, though. "Leona had told us, sort of in passing, that she was going to London," Margaret recalls. "She didn't go into any details. You have no idea what it's like to turn on the national news on TV and see your daughter in tears, in custody."

The scene quickly shifted from Leona's personal plight—her pregnancy was getting dangerously close to the eight-week mark at which RU486 can no longer be used—to a Brooklyn court, where the judge overturned the seizure. But the pills themselves remained in custody. Two weeks after the confiscation of the pills, U.S. Supreme Court Justice Clarence Thomas overruled the Brooklyn judge. Leona had another surgical abortion, "and glad I was to have it," she says.

Not long after that episode, 15-year-old Nyree Emory of New York City also found herself facing the dilemma of an unwanted, unplanned pregnancy. It was a full family dilemma: Nyree's 19-year-old sister, and the girlfriend of her 14-year-old cousin were all three in the same predicament. They would each make different choices.

Nyree's mother had warned repeatedly against pregnancy at a young age. "We weren't religious, and she wasn't strict," Nyree says today, "but having been a teen mom herself, and raising four children with my step-dad in the Bronx," she knew the perils. Meaning, specifically, "trying to keep us all alive, off drugs, out of jail and graduating high school...which she did, on a postal worker and a private school custodian's combined income. (But) adding another child, especially a baby, would have been too much of a financial burden, not to mention the overall burden on the family.

"My only option would have been to move out on my own, apply for public assistance and pretty much forget about finishing school. Sure, I could always go back, but the statistics (against that probability) are hard to argue with. I wasn't naïve at all; I saw my future very plainly if I didn't make that choice."

Nyree, a strikingly beautiful African American woman, told me her story on the sunny outdoor plaza of the Manhattan building that houses HBO, where she is an award winning associate producer for creative services. Her sister is a registered nurse living in a home she owns with her husband, happily raising pre-teen twin daughters. But the child she bore at that earlier time, now 23, "is expecting his own second child after having his first at 18, hasn't finished high school and is still working towards his GED," Nyree says. "His life...is a struggle, a stark contrast to the life my nieces now live. My cousin (whose girlfriend opted to have her baby at the same time Nyree chose otherwise ) is still with the mother of his child. They didn't move out of my aunt's house until about seven years ago, because they simply couldn't afford to."

Nyree tells the family story with no hint of disapproval or judgment, but simply because she is feels she made the right choice for herself and worries that the right to make that choice could disappear. After hearing of this book through a mutual friend she contacted me to offer her story. Nyree paid for her own education, is not married, has no children, "and generally I'm pretty damn happy with my life."

Encompassing both hard-luck stories and success stories, that particular family story is one of millions connected to reproductive rights and the ways that they play out today. Legal or not, easy or difficult to obtain, every abortion involves not just a fetus but also a woman—and often, in complex ways, a family.

# Chapter 12

# A Look Into the Future

In the year 3000, if humankind still exists, abortion will still exist. This will happen despite the fact that most of us, pro-choice, anti-abortion and uncommitted alike, would like to see the day when it no longer *does* happen. For those who would ban it entirely, nature will still arrange occasional abortions in the case of pregnancies that should not be, and common sense or the medical profession will still prevail in cases of egregious need—rape, incest or the imminent death of the mother. For those of us who believe it should be a woman's choice, there is widespread desire for it to be, as Rev. Scotty McLennan and others say, "safe, legal and rare," with the emphasis on "rare." That could happen. With widespread and improved sex education; accurate information about and availability of contraception; with strengthened women's health, better overall education and public healthcare, it could happen. Such a day is still far off.

Today in the United States abortion is theoretically safe and legal, but in many areas that applies only to women with money and resources. Women with money and resources can always simply board an airplane or get in their cars and drive to a safe place. But increasingly, women without power or necessary funds are finding it impossible to have the abortion they often desperately need. It is the plight of these women that motivates physicians like Willie Parker and the un-named other medical professionals in this book to take great risks in order to make safe, legal abortion available. It is their plight that motivates most of those who fight for keeping choice legal and it is their plight that motivates this writer, because I was one of them. I was not uneducated or, in the end, unable to come up with the funds for a crude, dangerous procedure; I simply had no choice for a safe and legal option. I survived. Thousands of women just like me died in those same years. We survivors, pro-choice activists and medical professionals hope to keep women from winding up maimed or dead from illegal abortions in the future.

Many medical professionals, though certainly not all, view abortion as an integral part of women's healthcare. Some limit the procedure strictly to cases of critical need such as saving the mother's life, some perform abortions only within the first trimester, some accept the broader issue of it being a woman's choice. Some, for political or religious reasons, do not perform abortions under any circumstances. However the struggle for and against reproductive freedom shifts in the future, these variations are likely always to exist. Although some long-time activists like Carol Downer and Judith Arcana, whose stories appear in earlier chapters, believe that non-professional—albeit carefully trained—women will step in to help other women if the legal right to abortion disappears, most Americans of any age would agree that having medical professionals in charge is a wiser and preferable option.

The probability that trained physicians will be available to perform abortions in the future is thanks in large part to the work of Jody Steinauer MD, MAS, and Medical Students for Choice, the organization she founded with a small group of then fellow students at the University of California San Francisco in 1993.

MSFC was formed in response to the virulent anti-choice movement of the 1980s and early 1990s. Shortly before the murder of Dr. David Gunn in Florida, tens of thousands of medical students all over the United States had received brochures, delivered to their home addresses, that the MSFC website sums up as conveying a breathtakingly offensive "joke." "Q: What would you do if you were in a room with Hitler, Mussolini and an abortionist and you had a gun with only two bullets? A: Shoot the abortionist twice." In addition to the increasing violence of the anti-choice movement, these students realized that many medical schools were not including abortion in their curricula, leaving new physicians unprepared to give competent counsel and advice on reproductive health to their patients. Many of these students were understandably conflicted about whether to offer abortion services as part of their practice. Steinauer and a small group of colleagues decided to take action with the formation of MSFC. They argued that abortion and reproductive health must be taught in medical schools and offered as residency training, and its providers supported, if women are to have reproductive choice. They also believed that the stigma must be removed. The success they have enjoyed thus far in terms of curriculum reform, expanded training opportunities and increased awareness of reproductive rights is likely to continue in years ahead. From the handful of students who gathered to organize in 1993, MSFC has grown into an internationally recognized nonprofit with a network of more than 10,000 medical students and residents in North America and abroad. Noting that less than one fourth of the counties in the U.S. today have a trained abortion provider and a majority of those providers, wherever they do exist, are over 50, MSFC hopes to improve both of those statistics.

Karen Meckstroth, MD, MPH is among those on the frontline in the training of tomorrow's doctors. An associate professor in the Department of Obstetrics, Gynecology and Reproductive Health at the University of California San Francisco, Meckstroth also serves as medical director of the Women's Options Center, Mt. Zion, and the Women's Community Clinic. She is concerned not only about education and training of new physicians, but also about the obstacles to reproductive freedom. "There are laws that punish women, such as Utah's requirement of a 72-hour waiting period and further attempts to criminalize the procedure there, and laws that allow physicians to lie to their patients such as in Kansas and elsewhere when the doctor may withhold information about fetal anomalies because he or she fears the woman might choose to have an abortion." Meckstroth begins her classes with an overview of restrictive laws across the U.S. and some hard data on who winds up suffering from these restrictions. "Poor women are disproportionately affected for a long list of reasons, including lack of access, travel and childcare issues, and inability to take time off from work."

Meckstroth credits the UCSF-based research and health policy think tank ANSIRH—Advancing New Standards in Reproductive

Health—with developing data and policy information to help prepare her students for tomorrow. Founded in 2002 by Felicia Stewart, MD, and Tracy Weitz, PhD, MPA, the nonprofit includes clinicians, scholars and researchers in a wide variety of health, economics and legal fields. ANSIRH maintains that reproductive care and health policy should be dictated by science rather than politics and that it is mandatory always to be moving the field forward.

Others in teaching and in reproductive rights activism cite the ongoing work of the Guttmacher Institute, an independent nonprofit founded in 1968 to provide research, policy analysis and education in fields relating to reproductive health. Named in honor of distinguished obstetrician-gynecologist Alan F. Guttmacher (1898-1974,) the Institute has offices in Washington D.C. and New York. "We may be the foot soldiers in the battle for reproductive rights," commented one medical school professor, "but Guttmacher is the Department of the Army and Department of Defense combined." This same professor directed me to the tribute to its namesake on the Guttmacher website which includes this description: *He was enraged by injustice and hypocrisy and impatient with the glacial pace of progress; yet he knew that each fear of change, however irrational, must be dealt with and that a revolution is composed of a thousand steps, most of them small.* And this quotation from Alan Guttmacher himself: "We really have the opportunity now to extend free choice in family planning to all Americans, regardless of social status, and to demonstrate to the rest of the world how it can be done. It's time we got on with the job."

Dr. Smith (a pseudonym), an abortion provider in a state where access is heavily restricted, sees family planning as critical and believes those who interfere – legislators and others – "are practicing medicine without a license." Dr. Smith says the consequences of layered restrictions and lack of access to reproductive care "leave many women no choice but to parent unwanted children, who then often suffer along with the rest of an overburdened family. Most women know that if they can get to a Planned Parenthood clinic it's a safety net, but the money could go away – and then we'll see all the negative consequences of unwanted pregnancies." Are we seeing them now? "Not yet. But I really, really worry that it's coming. Especially with the high rate of teen pregnancies, and especially among the immigrant population."

Dr. Smith admits to the occasional temptation simply to go somewhere else, take up another kind of practice. But he remains committed to reproductive rights and he loves what he does. "What I don't love, what makes me most angry, is why anybody thinks they have the right to tell anyone else what to do with her own body. And the hypocrisy, because this comes from the 'less government' people." His fear is that more laws, more restrictions and decreasing access will make increased numbers of unwanted children and all the attendant problems a reality. Smith returns again and again to his number one theme: abortion, and many other issues, would become non-issues if effective family planning could be maintained.

All of these supporters of reproductive rights—teachers, providers, activists, policy wonks alike—see the future not in terms of unlimited abortion, though they all believe in a woman's right to choose, but in terms of education, prevention, contraception, birth control...and family planning. Many of those I spoke with in developing stories and materials for this book lamented the multiple, sometimes overlapping, organizations working to support reproductive rights in the U.S. Ultimately, though, there is common support for the overarching goal of a comprehensive program. Such a program, they believe, would make abortion rare.

They would get agreement from Floris, who shared the story of an abortion she had at 18. She is now married and the mother of a six-year-old son. Floris and her husband do not want any more children, which poses no problem because they both have good jobs and can afford birth control. When they were sexually active 12 years ago, though, they had no access to birth control, something that still angers her. She told me, "I had tried so hard to get birth control and couldn't. The nearest Planned Parenthood clinic was hundreds of miles away from where I lived. I didn't have any money at all. My boyfriend, who is now my husband, and I were as careful as possible but I still got pregnant." Floris directs her anger at "the system" which she believes failed her. "It's expensive, you know? If you can't afford a private doctor, and there isn't any public health clinic to turn to like Planned Parenthood, then when you're 18 you don't know anything about contraception and you're just likely to get pregnant. I had to end a pregnancy that I feel like should never have happened." Floris' line of reasoning is certainly open to question, but it sheds light on the dilemma of young women in areas without access to public health centers. And it reinforces the argument that education and birth control could reduce the incidence of abortion—the ending of those pregnancies "that should never have happened."

Earlier chapters have offered glimpses of those who have brought reproductive rights to the forefront, and stories of some who are speaking out today. But one other thread is common: despite arguments for choice that are being made daily in newspapers and magazines, on blogs and social media sites, in legislatures and at community events, the stigma attached to abortion still keeps it closeted. And the closet keeps the very real faces of women—and men—involved from being seen or their voices from being heard. If change is to come, the door must open at least enough for light to shine in. One friend, not long after I started this project, told of bringing up the subject after an exercise class, when she and a group of friends regularly adjourn to a nearby deli for coffee and conversation. Out of nine women mostly in their 40s and 50s, four had had abortions. Two of these took place after marriage and family were established; the other two had happened when the women were in their teens and did not feel ready or able to bear a child. In every case, pregnancy had occurred despite use of one or more forms of birth control. None of the women had spoken of the experience to anyone other than immediate family (and in two cases to one or more close friends.) At my request, the friend later asked her fellow fitness buffs why they had essentially kept their abortions secret. The consensus was, she reported, that "you just don't. You don't mention it. Some people will be critical or judgmental, and no one can possibly understand without your going into more detail than you want."

Our family friend Jeanette would fit right in with the exercise class group:

We had just finished a leisurely dinner of pork tenderloin and applesauce, a casual evening of good wine, good conversation and good friends. The conversation during dinner turned, as conversations at our dinner table tended to do for at least a year or two before this book was completed, to the subject of abortion. Afterwards Jeanette, who is in her early 40s, bright, lively, elfin pretty and a successful businesswoman, drew me aside. Jeanette has never married, though she has had an assortment of relationships I've never quite been able to track. "I need to talk to you," she whispered, "I've had an abortion myself." It was as if she were confessing to an unreported federal crime. "I've never told anyone before."

By any measure, we've come a long way in the U.S. since Madame Restell went to jail for providing abortions to 19th century New York society and Margaret Sanger was moved to action by the horrors she saw from botched attempts to self-abort. My lovely young friend was able to have a perfectly legal abortion for an unintended pregnancy. But she only mentions it in whispers. Shame and guilt are still frequently associated with making the choice; secrecy is the norm. "On the personal level," remarked one young, female Ob-Gyn, "abortion remains 'the unspeakable,' and I think that's a very bad thing. We can talk about mastectomies and contraceptives and all manner of intimate sexual activities, but we can't talk about having an abortion. On one level I understand this, because the decision is quite personal and complex. I certainly don't tell my patients they ought to go around telling the world about their abortions. But I'm afraid if women don't start talking about it we will lose both the right and the attendant dignity everyone deserves."

Nancy Keenan agrees that openness and dialog are needed. Keenan took over the presidency of NARAL Pro-Choice America (founded as the National Abortion and Reproductive Rights Action League) in 2004, spearheading the pro-choice movement for nearly a decade before announcing her decision to step down at the end of 2012. She is credited with expanding the debate to include a focus on prevention of unwanted pregnancies, aligning herself with most in the reproductive rights camp and even some in the anti-abortion camp who hope eventually to see the procedure as safe, legal and—that key word again—rare. But Keenan, a former member of the Montana State House of Representatives who was named one of Washington's 100 most powerful women by *Washingtonian Magazine* in 2006, is fierce in her stance that abortion is and must remain personal, private and a woman's right. She is both realistic and optimistic about the future.

"Susan Wicklund (an Ob-Gyn whose story is included in the preceding chapter) had a young woman patient who had come all the way from Wyoming to Montana for an abortion," Keenan says. "The woman was driven by a friend who never knew the intent of the trip, but was told it was for a job interview. This is the sort of silence that must end. The movement has got to change. We have got to talk about (the issue) in terms of the stories, which opponents to reproductive rights don't want to hear. There is one commonality pre and post-Roe: the shame. People are ambiguous, and that's okay. But it is among the most common procedures in women's medicine, it is morally complex, and yet there is stigma and shame."

Keenan doesn't expect Roe v. Wade to be overturned—although she continues to fight hard for political candidates who support the law—but she also is realistic about the loss of reproductive rights that disempowered women are experiencing in many areas right now. "It's no longer about what's legal," she notes, "but about what's accessible."

Still, she is optimistic. "Looking ahead, I really do have hope. The millennial generation, those born between 1981 and 1999, children of the baby boomers are the largest generation ever. There are 76 million of them. They are the tipping point of the movement. They are diverse, racially and ethnically. They are urban—three out of four of them live in a city or a suburb. They are very well educated and they value education highly. They are fiercely independent. They're getting married and having children later in life than in any previous generation. They are tech-savvy, and they communicate to a global audience. While we had friends in the neighborhood; they have friends in the world. And the majority of them are pro-choice. We have to get them to understand this right can be lost."

Despite the intensity of opposition to abortion, and the fact that no generation can fit neatly into one box, Keenan believes the millennials will ensure the future of reproductive rights. Their generational characteristics, she maintains, are compatible with the support of reproductive freedom. "They vote social justice. And by 2020, 40 per cent of eligible voters in the U.S. will be millennials. Along with so many others today, they understand that abortion is integral to women's health, and is a personal right."

Cecile Richards is also optimistic. For Richards, who took over as president of Planned Parenthood Federation of America and the Planned Parenthood Action Fund in 2006, optimism would seem hard to come by. Planned Parenthood clinics are regularly targeted by anti-abortion protesters; and the organization itself, despite the varied and significant services it provides in education and health benefits especially to low-income Americans, is under constant threat from legislators and right-wing activists because some of its clinics also provide abortions. But Richards, a Democratic Party activist and the daughter of former Texas governor Ann Richards, looks at what her organization does in its work "for a healthier and safer world for women and teens" with pride—and hope. She offered the following comment on the future of reproductive rights in September, 2012, shortly after delivering a wildly-applauded speech at the Democratic convention. (Nancy Keenan also spoke at the convention, to repeated standing ovations.)

"My mom raised me with the belief that you never turn down a new opportunity," Richards says. "There's always going to be a reason to say no—you don't have the right clothes, right degree, right experience, right connections. And I certainly had those thoughts when I was offered the job to lead Planned Parenthood. But I followed my mom's advice and said yes. It was such an amazing opportunity—I'd always been a supporter and knew if I joined, I'd have the chance to work on behalf of issues I care deeply about.

"The job has been nonstop since I took it six years ago. We've faced unprecedented challenges—the political attacks just keep coming. But throughout all these challenges, I hear every day from patients who tell me about how Planned Parenthood helped them. For some, it's that one of our health centers was the only place they could go for birth control. Or that they came to us when they were afraid to talk to their parents or friends about a health concern. I hear from women whose lives were saved because of our cancer screenings. These stories propel me through some of our hardest fights. At the end of the day, I know we're on the right side of these issues, and I want to make sure the three million men and women who rely on us will always have access to our health care services.

"Something that has increasingly given me hope is seeing how much young people are getting involved in what we do. In the past year and a half, we've gained 1.5 million new supporters—half of them are young, and most are registered to vote. These young people see what's happening to women's access to health care, and they don't like it. They're helping lead our movement. They come out to our rallies—they register their friends to vote—they've started pro-women health groups on their campuses—they're energized. They are fighting for their own access to health care. Because this is about their autonomy—their ability to make their own health care decisions so they can have the future they want."

The stories of this book, other than those about women going outside our borders to access safe procedures, focus on the situation in the U.S. But just as the millennials are a globally-focused generation, abortion is a global concern. In most European countries today women may choose to have an abortion, though circumstances vary. In Ireland it is legal only if the mother's life is in danger. In Africa, over five million women annually risk their lives by trying to end a pregnancy, without medical help and often under unsafe conditions. In Liechtenstein an abortion is punishable by one year in prison—and it's not the man involved who serves out the term. In the U.S., according to a 2011 report by the Guttmacher Institute, 162 abortion-restricting laws were passed in 19 states in that one year alone.

It may be that our future, if the millennials don't pitch in to shape it differently, is not much more than a rehash of our past, those brutal times that spurred Margaret Sanger to action. It is worth remembering that what she sought was not unlimited abortion but widespread family planning. Plenty of brutality is still around. It was evident in 2011/12 in testimony about the Women's Medical Society Clinic in West Philadelphia, Pennsylvania—blood and filth everywhere, patients winding up injured or with venereal disease—during the investigation of Dr. Kermit Gosnell on federal drug charges and the murder of one patient in 2009. Anti-abortion forces blamed the pro-choice community for opposing inspections; pro-choice forces said nothing was done when inspections had in fact shown serious problems. Would women ever have gone to the clinic if there had not been extensive state restrictions, or if funding for low-income women had been available? That's a question without an answer. A different kind of brutality is seen in stories told by women who went to "pregnancy counseling centers" that they thought offered comprehensive services, only to hear themselves called "baby-killer" when they mentioned they were considering an abortion. Many such centers provide compassionate care and valuable services—but so do Planned Parenthood health centers, where as often as not, one must pass through a metal detector at the door. The loudest voices of anti-abortion forces say life begins at the moment of conception and even the "morning-after" pill is murder. The staunchest among the pro-choice hold that no one should dictate to a woman what she can do with her own body.

These stark facts belong to the past and the present: Tragedies v. desperate women. Compassionate care v. humiliation, or no care at all. Family planning v. unwanted children. Womb v. soul. Baby killer v. woman hater. As long as one side only shouts at the other the same battles will be waged into the future, because abortion is not going to disappear. And emotions quickly overrule reason.

What if common ground could be sought? Mutual respect, healthy families, better understanding of differing points of view? No one wants to see increased numbers of unwanted children or sick and maimed women. Most want women to have at least some degree of autonomy and the poor to have some protection. Perhaps the ample common ground might even support movement toward a stronger, healthier country. And the history of brutality won't repeat itself.

One can hope.

CPSIA information can be obtained at www.ICGtesting.com
Printed in the USA
LVOW01s1908030614

388412LV00002B/4/P

9 781936 411221